Dolphins
& Whales

Dolphins & Whales

STEPHEN SAVAGE

Eagle Editions

A QUANTUM BOOK

Published by Eagle Editions Ltd
11 Heathfield
Royston
Hertfordshire SG8 5BW

Copyright ©MCMXCI
Quintet Publishing plc

This edition printed 2003

ISBN 1-86160-667-2

QUMVAD

This book is produced by
Quantum Publishing Ltd
6 Blundell Street
London N7 9BH

Typeset in Great Britain by
Central Southern Typesetters, Eastbourne
Manufactured in Hong Kong by
Regent Publishing Services Limited
Printed in Singapore by
Star Standard Industries (Pte) Ltd

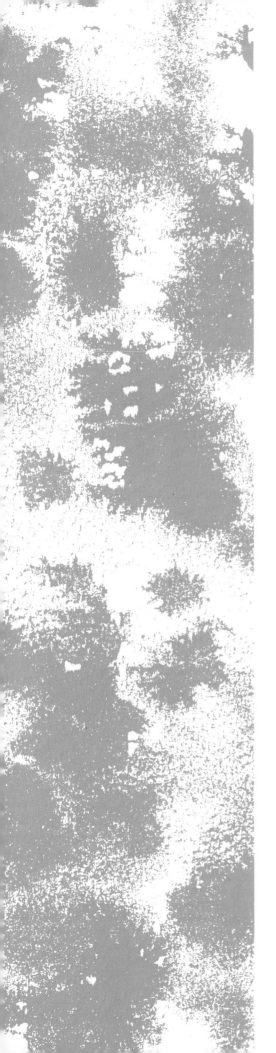

CONTENTS

ABOVE: The common porpoise usually travels in small groups and can often be seen near the shore or riding the bow wave of a ship. They are also known as the harbour porpoise, because they are often seen in harbours and estuaries.

INTRODUCTION

LEFT: A humpback whale diving whilst in its feeding grounds, off the coast of Alaska. These whales have coarse baleen and feed on small fish such as anchovy and caplin.

RIGHT: This illustration is from *The Natural History of Fishes and Serpents Volume III*, by R. Brookes, published in 1763. It includes a depiction of the Fin Fish, which this book says is 'as long as a Whale, but is three times less in bulk. It is known by the fin on the back near the tail, and by its spouting up the water more violently and higher than the whale.'

Whale?

6

Fin-Fish.

11

Porpoise?

24

Dolphin of the Antients.

26

Whales and dolphins have captured the human imagination since they were first described by Aristotle the Greek philosopher and natural scientist in the fourth century BC. Aristotle was probably the first person to classify whales and dolphins as mammals, rather than fish. It was to be many centuries, however, before most of the whale and dolphin species that we know today were recognized. Even so, we know very little about these mysterious fish-like mammals and scientists are still at odds over whether there are 77, 78 or 80 different species.

Whales and dolphins belong to a group of animals called Cetacea, from the Greek word *cetus*, meaning whale. The larger cetaceans, measuring over 4–5 m (13–16 ft), are known as whales, and the smaller cetaceans are called dolphins and porpoises. All cetaceans are air-breathing mammals which spend their entire lives in water. They number some of the largest animals that have ever existed. In fact the largest species, the blue whale (*Balaenoptera musculus*), is twice the length of the biggest known dinosaur.

Probably the best-known species of cetacean is the bottlenosed dolphin (*Tursiops truncatus*), which has been popularized by television programmes such as *Flipper*. Flipper, who was played by more than just one dolphin, soon became a household name, and remains so today. However, this was a marked change from previous films featuring cetaceans where people risked life and limb to hunt the 'fearsome' whales in the frozen waters of the Antarctic. The bottlenosed dolphin is also the species most frequently seen in marine parks and dolphinaria. These marine zoos have played an important role in changing our attitudes towards cetaceans and the life beneath the sea, which before was inaccessible and virtually unknown.

Very few people who have seen a whale or dolphin can remain untouched by the almost magical aura that sur-rounds them. Throughout the ages they have inspired our poets, musicians and artists. We marvel at their complete mastery of their watery world, a world where they live in harmony. Although they seem to possess some human characteristics, the need to kill and destroy their world is thankfully not among them. We have hunted whales for centuries and it is only now, with many species on the edge of extinction, that we see them through different eyes. But today they have to face what may well be the greatest threat to their existence yet: the polychlorinated biphenyls (PCBs) and other toxic chemicals that we have flushed into the oceans – the silent, invisible killers.

BELOW: Early sightings of sea serpents may have actually been glimpses of groups of porpoises. This engraving is from *The Natural History of Norway* by Rev. Erich Pontoppidon, published in 1755.

A LIFE
IN WATER

LEFT: A
Mediterranean
dolphin breaks the
surface of the water.

Mesonyx, from 50 million years ago, had the robust and comparatively unspecialised skull of a carnivorous mammal.

Within 5 million years, the protocetids were displaying numerous adaptations to marine life, most significantly in the lengthening of the 'beak'.

The dorudontines were well adapted to life in the sea by 40 million years ago. The nostrils were moving back and a definite 'beak' had formed.

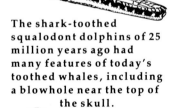

The shark-toothed squalodont dolphins of 25 million years ago had many features of today's toothed whales, including a blowhole near the top of the skull.

15 million years ago modern dolphins appeared

To appreciate the many whale and dolphin species that are known today, it is important to understand something of their origin.

The order Cetacea is divided into three suborders: the Archaeoceti – extinct primitive cetaceans; the Odontoceti – toothed whales; and the Mysticeti – filter-feeding or baleen whales. Although fossil records show that the Archaeoceti were the first to appear, they are not thought to be the ancestors of either the toothed whales or the baleen whales and no earlier fossils have yet been found. The Archaeoceti abounded in the middle Eocene epoch (around 45 million years ago), with a few persisting into the Miocene epoch (5–24 million years ago). The first Odontoceti appeared in the late Eocene epoch and spread rapidly during the middle Miocene epoch (about 15 million years ago). The Mysticeti didn't appear until much later, and were unknown before the middle Oligocene epoch (30 million years ago). The earliest members of this suborder were the cetothers, which even at this early stage showed distinctive Mysticeti features. It is not known from what land animal they evolved, but it seems likely that it was some toothed mammal.

As whales and dolphins adapted to an aquatic lifestyle, they reverted back to the streamlined forms of earlier marine creatures. The forelimbs became modified into flippers which were (and still are) used for steering and balance. The flippers, or pectoral fins, contain a similar arrangement of bones to those present in land mammals – another indicator of their land-based ancestry. Most species have a dorsal fin on the upper surface of the body, which is used for balance. It is not attached by bone, but is well supplied with blood vessels which may also aid the control of body heat. The large tail, or caudal fin, which is used as the main source of propulsion, is horizontally flattened, instead of being held vertically, as in fish. The caudal vertebrae extend down through the centre of the tail, almost to the end. The fluke (lobe of the tail) itself is not supported by bone, but is composed of strong connective tissue. There is no external evidence of hind limbs, but some species possess two elongated slender bones which represent the vestigial pelvis. The cetacean skull also has changed greatly from that of land mammals. The nostril, or blowhole, has moved to the top of the head, allowing cetaceans to breathe at the surface of the water without making themselves too visible.

The cetacean body is enclosed in blubber, which may account for 30–40% of a whale's body weight and be up to 60 cm (24 in) thick. The thickness of the blubber not only depends on the species, body size, and availability of food, but may also be affected by the season, migration and whether or not the whale is lactating. The thickness of

BELOW: As early as the 18th century, scientists were attempting to depict the variety of skull forms of whales and dolphins, as in this table from *Theatrum Universale Omnium Animalium,* published in 1718.

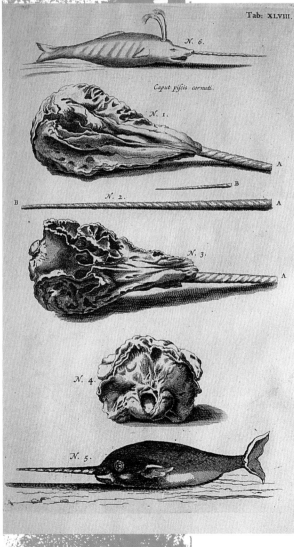

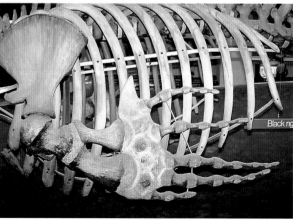

RIGHT: The arrangement of bones in the cetacean flipper is very similar to that in the limbs of land mammals. It is easy to understand why scientists believe that the ancestors of whales and dolphins once lived on land.

the blubber will also vary on different parts of the body. The blubber has two main functions: firstly as an insulative layer to reduce the amount of body heat lost to the water; and secondly, as a source of food. It is only loosely attached to the rest of the body and is easily stripped away by whalers.

The skin of cetaceans is very thin by comparison and is thought to be quite sensitive. Both whales and dolphins have frequently been seen exploring

LEFT: Spotted dolphins and diver. A human diver looks ungainly in the water when compared with the aquatic adaptation of the dolphin.

BELOW: The dolphin is perfectly adapted to an aquatic existence. The pectoral fins are used for steering and the dorsal fin acts rather like the keel on the underside of a yacht.

objects by rubbing their bodies against them. Cetaceans in marine zoos certainly enjoy being stroked and often rub themselves against an outstretched hand. Cetaceans have no hair except for a few bristles present on some species, which are thought to have a sensory function. Whales and dolphins have a special gland at the corner of their eyes which secretes a thick oily fluid that lubricates the eyes and protects them from the salt water. The external ears have become reduced to a small pin prick filled with wax. Most sound is received through the lower jaw (see Chapter 3).

In spite of being the ultimate adaptation to an aquatic environment, they are still tied to the surface world by their need for air. Even so, they are able to remain submerged for much longer periods than humans are able to. Although it seems obvious, the lungs of whales are much larger than those of humans. However, their body size is also much greater, so proportionately there is not a huge difference. The secret lies in their ability to utilize the oxygen more fully. When humans breathe they only absorb about 20% of the oxygen inhaled, but the bottlenosed dolphin (*Tursiops truncatus*) uses 80% and the great whales may use up to 90%. Whales and dolphins are also able to store oxygen in their muscles which can be used later when diving. The

ABOVE: Although adult dolphins possess no hair, this mammalian characteristic is visible on the beak of a new-born dolphin calf, and on the heads of some baleen whales.

ABOVE: The dolphin is thought to have eyesight equivalent to that of a horse. The reflective inner surface of their eyes allows them to see quite well in low light conditions.

length of time a cetacean can stay submerged differs greatly between species. The bottlenosed dolphin is a coastal species and can remain underwater for seven minutes, although it usually surfaces more frequently. Being a coastal animal it does not have to undertake deep excursions to search for food. On the other hand, the sperm whale (*Physeter macrocephalus*) can dive to a depth of over 3,000 m (10,000 ft) in search of prey and can hold its breath for over an hour.

Whales and dolphins can also return from deep dives without suffering from a condition known as 'the bends'. Human divers breathe compressed air and under pressure nitrogen becomes dissolved in the blood. If a diver ascends from the depths too quickly and without decompression, nitrogen bubbles form in the body causing great pain and possibly permanent damage. It is thought that whales avoid this by absorbing nitrogen into an oily substance, thus averting the dangers risked by human divers.

Cetaceans are also excellent swimmers and some species can achieve relatively high speeds. The fastest-

swimming marine mammal is the killer whale (*Orcinus orca*), which can reach a top speed of 55 kph (35 mph). Many other toothed whale species can achieve astonishing bursts of speed. The larger baleen whales usually swim much more slowly. For example, the blue whale usually swims at 6–8 kph (3.7–5.0 mph), and can only sustain faster speeds for short periods. The rorquals, which include the blue whale (*Balaenoptera musculus*), the sei whale (*B. borealis*) and the minke whale (*B. acutorostrata*), are the speedsters of the baleen whales.

Bow riding is a well-known behaviour exhibited by dolphins and porpoises. Many species, such as the common dolphin (*Delphinus delphis*) and the dusky dolphin (*Lagenorhynchus obscurus*), seem to delight in riding the bow wave produced at the front of a ship, which in effect pushes the dolphin through the water. There is often much jostling for a position on the wave and the dolphins may cast an inquisitive eye at the enthralled onlookers on deck.

Many people do not know the difference between a dolphin and a porpoise. This is not made any easier by the existence of a dolphin fish, and the American custom of calling all dolphins porpoises. True porpoises belong only to the family Phocoenidae. They have stubby bodies, no beak (narrow snout), and spade-like teeth. The best-known species is the common porpoise (*Phocoena phocoena*), which may reach 1.8 m (6 ft) in length and weigh up to 90 kg (200 lb). Porpoises are usually classified as the smallest group of whales.

It is not fully understood why cetaceans returned to the sea all those

millions of years ago, but competition for space and food were probably important factors. It is thought that the toothed whales and the baleen whales did not evolve from a common ancestor, but instead were a result of parallel evolution, when two individual animal groups solved the problems of adapting to the same environment in a similar way. Cetaceans have three parts to their stomachs, as do land herbivores, and it is therefore assumed that the cetaceans' ancestors were herbivorous. These early ancestors may have grazed on aquatic plants or hunted primitive fish in the shallow waters.

The search for food is an important part of any animal's life, and is no less important to cetaceans. However, toothed whales and baleen whales tackle the problem in different ways. Baleen whales no longer possess teeth. Instead

ABOVE: Baleen whales have no teeth, but instead sieve the oceans for tiny shoaling fish and crustaceans, trapping them with fibrous baleen plates which hang from their upper jaw.

RIGHT: This beautifully coloured plate is from *Giant Fishes, Whales and Dolphins* by J. R. Norman and F. C. Fraser, published in 1937. It represents an accurate portrayal ofthe blue whale and the humpback whale.

they have developed baleen plates which are attached to the top half of the jaw and used to sieve the water for food. A baleen plate is a horny structure containing keratin, similar to the horny growths of land animals such as nails, claws and feathers. Some baleen whales have quite fine baleen and feed on small invertebrates, including shrimp-like crustaceans called krill. The blue whale and the sei whale have fine baleen. Other species, including the minke whale, have a much coarser baleen, and include small fish in their diet. Baleen whales also use different methods of catching their prey. The right whale (*Eubalaena glacialis*) swims near the surface and sieves the water for tiny invertebrates. The blue whale lunges through the water, feeding mainly on krill, and the grey whale (*Eschrichtius robustus*) is a bottom feeder, ploughing up the bottom silt to feed on large crustaceans and molluscs. The humpback whale (*Megaptera novaeangliae*) has devised a unique way of catching small fish. Starting at a depth of about 15 m (50 ft), it slowly rises to the surface. As the whale spirals upwards, it forces air through its blowhole to create a screen of bubbles which forces its prey into a decreasingly smaller area. The whale then lunges up through the centre of the bubble net, engulfing large quantities of fish. This is probably the most spectacular feeding method of any cetacean. The humpback whale seems to be the only species to use this technique. Some baleen whales, the rorquals in particular, have a series of grooves

ABOVE: Killer whales may feed on marine mammals as well as fish, and killer whales have been known to take young sea-lions from the beach, an ability clearly demonstrated by Shamu at Sea World, Florida.

RIGHT: The humpback whale receives its name from the humped appearance of its back when diving. The air expelled from its blow hole may travel at 500 km per hour (300mph).

DOLPHINS
AND WHALES

20

which extend down the body from just below the mouth. Although their function is not clear, it is thought that they may allow expansion of the throat to aid swallowing.

Toothed whales and dolphins feed mainly on fish and squid. Most species possess sharp pointed teeth which are used to grasp and hold their prey, which is then swallowed whole. Killer whales are the exception, because they feed on seals, penguins and other cetaceans. The prey taken depends largely on what is available. The killer whale's fearsome reputation originated from stories told by early sailors, and has persisted to this day. There is, however, no evidence to show that a killer whale has ever attacked a human. Again,

marine zoos have been instrumental in showing the killer whale's true nature. However, they do hunt with amazing coordination, whatever the prey. They have also been known to almost beach themselves while taking a young sealion from shore.

The largest of the toothed whales is the sperm whale (*Physeter macrocephalus*), which is able to reach a length of 20 m (66 ft). The sperm whale's head may account for about a third of its overall length. It only has teeth in its lower jaw, and when the mouth is closed, the teeth fit into special sockets in the top half of the jaw. The diet of sperm whales seems to consist mainly of squid. These may be small open-water species, or giant squids from the hidden depths

BELOW: The sperm whale only possesses teeth in its upper jaw. The spermaceti organ, in the whale's head, is thought to be a lens to focus sound for echolocation, and to aid buoyancy at varying depths.

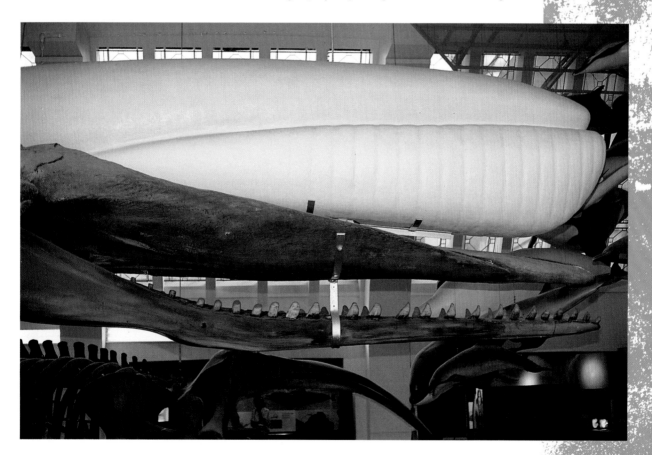

of the ocean. Circular scars present on the heads of large sperm whales are assumed to be the resulting evidence of a clash between titans.

Cetaceans do not need to drink fresh water. They are able to extract all the fresh water they need from their food and from salt water, swallowed during feeding. As only a few species of dolphin live in fresh water, this must have been an important factor in their adaptation to an aquatic environment.

Another problem that needed to be overcome during the course of evolution was that of sleep. Seals and sealions usually sleep on land, often congregating in large herds for protection. Whales and dolphins, however, must sleep in the water, but how they do this is not fully understood. All cetaceans need to breathe air, so a deep sleep as we know it would surely result in the cetacean drowning. It seems more likely that they 'cat nap' at the surface, being awake enough to continue breathing. It has also been suggested that cetaceans can rest one half of their brain at a time, enabling important functions such as breathing to continue. Dolphins that have been studied in marine zoos have been observed, day and night, slowly swimming around the pool with one eye closed, possibly indicating that they are resting one half of their brain. They have also been observed resting at the surface of the water for short periods of time.

BELOW: The dolphin's body is totally streamlined, enabling them to reach speeds of around 36.6 km per hour (22mph). Dolphins propel themselves through the water with vertical strokes of their tail.

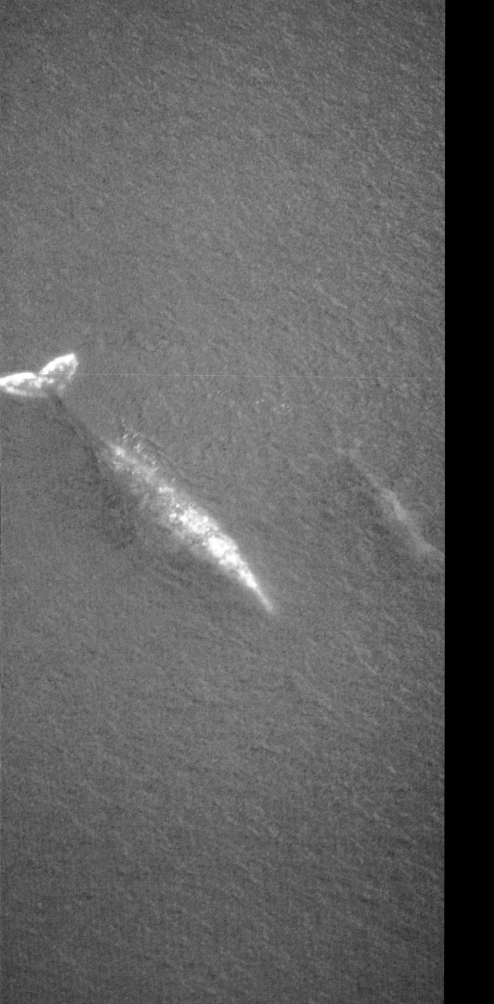

THE SOCIAL UNIT AND CARE OF THE YOUNG

LEFT: Whales and dolphins are warm-blooded mammals that give birth in the water to fully formed young. A grey whale calf is born after a 13 month gestation period and weighs 1,500kg (3,300lb).

ABOVE: The killer whale's true nature is far from that of the ruthless loner often portrayed. In fact, the killer whale lives in a very close social unit which may number 18 whales of varying ages.

Whales and dolphins are highly social animals that live in various types of group, the type varying between species. The strongest social unit is the family unit which may be small, as in many baleen whale species, or large, as in the killer whale (*Orcinus orca*), whose social unit averages 18 members. A typical killer whale unit consists of eight females, seven calves of various ages, and three adult males who are often related to one or other of the females.

There are many more species of toothed whale than there are baleen whales, so it stands to reason that the social structure of toothed whales should be more varied. Some species seem to be almost solitary, while others form great herds. The spinner dolphin (*Stenella longirostris*) and the common dolphin (*Delphinus delphis*) form large herds consisting of both sexes. However, the herd probably contains many smaller social units. Sperm whales (*Physeter macrocephalus*) have two distinctive social units, the harem and the bachelor herd. The harem, which is led by a single dominant bull, may contain 30 females, many of which may be pregnant or lactating a calf. The bachelor herds are usually much smaller and made up of immature males. The dominant harem bull will eventually be driven off by a younger, stronger male ensuring that the harem is always led by the strongest whale and only he will mate with the females.

The social structure of baleen whales seems to be confined to a few individuals, often consisting of three or four animals, as in the humpback whale. However, these small social units may be within the contact range of other scattered units, as the sounds produced by many baleen whales can travel many miles underwater, thus forming larger, loosely connected social groups. As their prey is very small, there is an obvious benefit for filter feeders if they are spread over a wide area, but most baleen whales congregate in large numbers in the breeding season. Baleen whales may have lived in much larger social units before whaling took its toll.

Some species of dolphin also live in small social groups such as the Yangtse River dolphin (*Lipotes vexillifer*), whose social group usually consists of 2–6 members, or the Amazon River dolphin (*Inia geoffrensis*), which is often found

ABOVE: The sperm whale is the largest of the toothed whale species, attaining a maximum length of 18m (60ft).

LEFT: A plate from *Historia Piscium Libri Quator* by Francisci Willughbell, published in 1686. The inscription at the bottom corner of the plate indicates that this plate was sponsored by Samuel Pepys, as were about half the plates in the book.

THE SOCIAL UNIT AND CARE OF THE YOUNG

ABOVE: 'Singing' male humpback whales compete for the opportunity to escort a single female whale in water between the Dominican Republic and Grand Turk.

in pairs. As with all river dolphin species, they merge into larger congregations at popular feeding sites or when drought conditions force them into the same area.

Some species of cetacean show great cooperation between members of the same social unit, particularly when feeding. Bottlenosed dolphins (*Tursiops truncatus*) have been observed feeding in a cooperative manner. Two or more dolphins from the school encircle a shoal of fish, herding them into a decreasingly smaller area. Other members of the school take turns to eat fish from the trapped shoal until all have had their share. Killer whales also cooperate in catching prey, which may help to strengthen the link between pod members (a pod is a stable group of

whales, often related to each other). This cooperation is not restricted to toothed whales. A pair of humpback whales (*Megaptera novae angliae*) will sometimes work together to catch small fish using the bubble net technique in a similar way to the dolphins.

Some species cooperate in other ways. Bottlenosed dolphins off Mauritania have been observed cooperating with local fishermen by helping to herd mullet into their nets. In so doing, they also increase their own catch by feeding on unwanted fish dumped by the fishermen. Whales and dolphins will also come to the aid of other group members in danger. Sperm whales will support another sick or injured pod member, as will bottlenosed dolphins. This behaviour is thought to have arisen

ABOVE OPPOSITE: A female bottlenosed dolphin and calf at Miami Seaquarium. Advances in animal husbandry have resulted in an increase in dolphin calves born and successfully reared in aquatic zoos and marine parks.

from the natural instinct of cetaceans to help their newborn calf to the surface for its first breath, and is demonstrated by all cetaceans to some degree. There have also been documented incidents where dolphins have supported a man in the water and saved him from drowning.

The strongest link shown by cetaceans is the maternal bond between mother and calf. Early whalers took advantage of this strong bond by harpooning a calf, knowing that the mother would not leave it, thus making her an easy target. Cetaceans have a long gestation period of about 12 months, which means that the newborn calf is fully formed and able to survive in the cold watery environment. Cetaceans give birth to a single calf which is fed on a very rich creamy milk. The calf grows up in the social unit and is protected

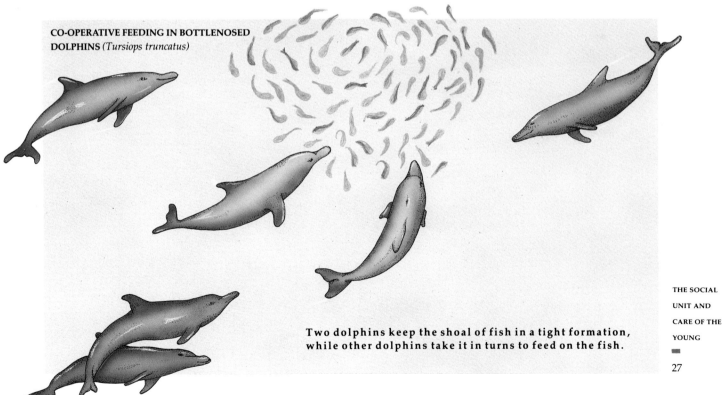

CO-OPERATIVE FEEDING IN BOTTLENOSED DOLPHINS (*Tursiops truncatus*)

Two dolphins keep the shoal of fish in a tight formation, while other dolphins take it in turns to feed on the fish.

and cared for until it is strong enough to fend for itself. Whether the calf remains with the unit or not depends on its sex and species.

With regard to birth and care of the young, the bottlenosed dolphin must rank as one of the better-documented cetaceans, as in the last few years there has been a great increase in the numbers of this species born in human care. A female bottlenosed dolphin becomes sexually mature at about 12 years old and may calve every second year. Gestation lasts 11–12 months, and most calves are born in spring and summer. At one time it was thought that calves were always born tail first. More recent research, however, has shown that head-first presentations are also common. As soon as the calf is born it swims to the surface to take its first breath. It may be assisted to the surface by one or more attendant females known as 'aunties'. The calf is about 1 m (3.3 ft) at birth, which is about a third the length of its mother. The calf is often darker than the mother and has several light vertical lines on its sides caused

BELOW: This illustration in Guillaume Rendelei'o *La Premiere Partie de l'Histoire Entiere des Poissons* (published 1558) shows an early awareness of the mammalian characteristics of dolphins, in that they gave birth to live offspring.

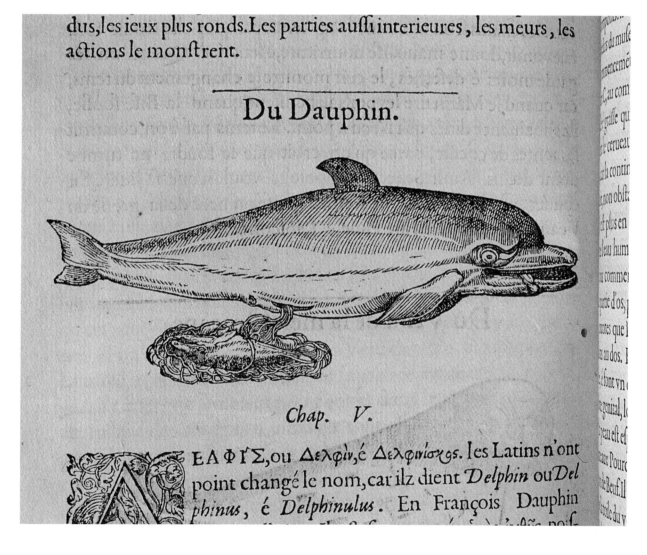

dus, les ieux plus ronds. Les parties aussi interieures, les meurs, les actions le monstrent.

Du Dauphin.

Chap. V.

ΕΑΦΥΣ, ou Δελφὶν, é Δελφινίσχϑς. les Latins n'ont point changé le nom, car ilz dient *Delphin* ou *Delphinus*, é *Delphinulus*. En François Dauphin

by the body being folded in the womb. These lines disappear after about a week.

Not long after the birth, the calf nuzzles its mother to be fed. The two nipples protrude through special slits on the underside of the female so that the calf can lock on to feed. The milk is thought to be under voluntary control by the mother and the calf is fed little and often. Dolphin milk is very rich and contains 20–30% fat and 10–16% protein, similar in composition to the blue whale's milk which contains approximately 38% fat and 12% protein. Human milk by comparison contains 3.5% fat, 1% protein and 6.5% lactose (milk sugar). Cetacean milk does not contain any lactose.

ABOVE: A one week old bottlenosed dolphin calf at the Brighton Dolphinarium in the UK. Like many new born mammals, its head is very pronounced at this stage.

RIGHT: A bottlenosed dolphin calf at the Brighton Dolphinarium in the UK, feeding on its mother's rich milk. A dolphin calf may suckle for 18 months before it is fully weaned onto fish.

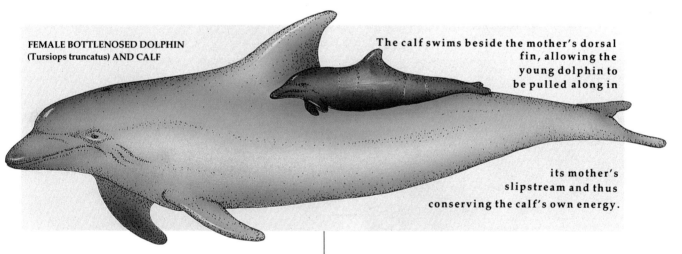

FEMALE BOTTLENOSED DOLPHIN
(Tursiops truncatus) AND CALF

The calf swims beside the mother's dorsal fin, allowing the young dolphin to be pulled along in

its mother's slipstream and thus conserving the calf's own energy.

LEFT: The common dolphin is possibly the most abundant species of dolphin worldwide. When travelling at high speed the common dolphin almost flies through the air whilst porpoising.

Studies done by the staff at the Brighton Dolphinarium (UK) indicate that the calf feeds regularly and often. Each feeding period may be broken down into actual sucklings, which only last a few seconds each. Intervals of about 20–30 minutes were observed in between these feeding periods where no suckling occurs. During these intervals, the calf may try to suckle, but the mother does not slow down and allow it to feed. The calf was observed feeding both day and night, but the suckling was noted to be less frequent at night. Many of these observations have also been made at other marine zoos.

Although the calf is fully formed, it spends most of the first few days stationed next to its mother's dorsal fin, as in this position it is pulled along in its mother's slipstream, allowing it to conserve its own energy. The mother steers the calf away from unfamiliar objects, and in marine zoos the mother steers the calf away from the pool sides until it is able to orientate itself. After a few days the calf is much stronger and changes position frequently, but still stays close to its mother. Care of the calf is often shared with the attending females. The maternal bond is continually re-affirmed by constant physical contact between mother and calf. If the calf ventures too far from its mother's side, she will rush after the calf and chastise it quite severely (by slapping it with her flukes or biting it). Life in the sea is harsh and a young calf is very vulnerable. The mortality rate of young dolphins is thought to be fairly high, particularly in the first few years. After a few years, the calf becomes more independent and is allowed to swim more freely. A bottlenosed dolphin calf may be suckled for about 18 months, although it usually starts to take some fish before it is a year old.

Some species of baleen whales undertake yearly migrations from their feeding grounds in polar waters to their breeding grounds in warmer waters. The grey whale (*Eschrichtius robustus*) begins its migration from its summer feeding grounds in arctic waters in early October. Their 20,000-km (12,400-mile) journey is thought to be the longest migration undertaken by any mammal. These whales are often visible from shore and the grey whale is the species most commonly seen by whale watchers on the west coast of the USA.

BELOW: A one month old bottlenosed dolphin calf at the Brighton Dolphinarium in the UK. Constant physical contact between mother and calf is very important in forming and strengthening the maternal bond.

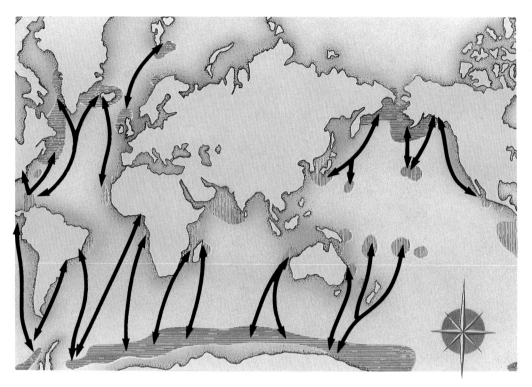

MIGRATION OF HUMPBACKS

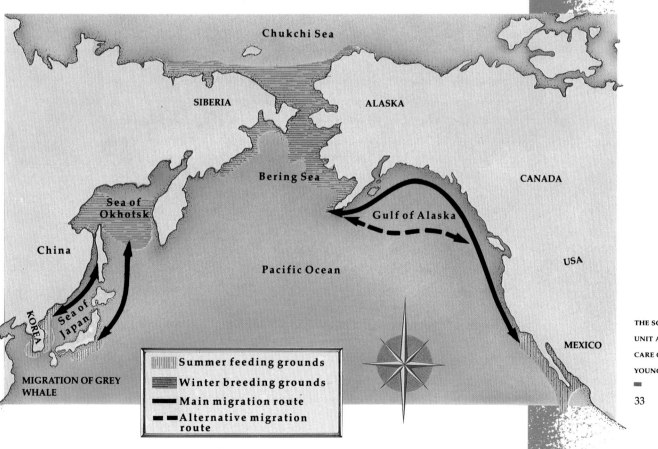

Chukchi Sea

SIBERIA   ALASKA

Bering Sea

CANADA

Sea of
Okhotsk

Gulf of Alaska

China

Pacific Ocean

USA

KOREA

Sea of
Japan

MEXICO

**MIGRATION OF GREY
WHALE**

	Summer feeding grounds
	Winter breeding grounds
	Main migration route
	Alternative migration route

The grey whales spend their winter in the lagoons around Baja, California and the Gulf of California, where they can calve in relative safety. Unlike the bottlenosed dolphin, baleen whales are usually unattended during calving. A newborn grey whale calf weighs about 1,500 kg (3,300 lb) and is 4.5 m (15 ft) in length. The blubber is relatively thin at this stage and would not provide adequate protection against the cold arctic waters. The maternal bond between mother and calf is established in the safety of the lagoon where it is fed by its mother. By the time the calf reaches arctic waters on the return journey, its blubber will be thick enough to protect it against the freezing temperatures. The calf is weaned at about seven months.

Another species that migrates is the humpback whale (*Legaptera novaeangliae*), which travels from its polar-water feeding grounds to warmer waters such as the Caribbean. Here the females calve and mate for the following year. The gestation period is about 12 months. A newborn calf weighs 2,500 kg (5,500 lb) and may put on 45 kg (100 lb) in weight each day. Like the grey whales, humpbacks may fast for up to eight months during this time.

But it is not only baleen whales that undertake such migrations. Many species of toothed whale, including beluga whales (*Delphinapterus leucas*),

ABOVE: Along the pacific coast of the US whale watchers avidly await the annual migration of the grey whales. Grey whales may fast for up to eight months during their migration.

sperm whales *(Physeter macrocephalus)* and the dusky dolphin *(Lagenorhynchus obscurus)* also migrate in this way, although their migrations do not match the great distances travelled by the grey whales. Many species of cetacean undertake short excursions as they follow the migration of their prey.

Dolphins seem to be the most playful of all the cetaceans, the bottlenosed dolphin being particularly so, and is the species most frequently involved in dolphin/human encounters. Dolphins have been observed surfing at sea, or bow riding, and sometimes leaping free of the water (breaching) close to boats, a behaviour exhibited most often by solitary, so-called friendly dolphins.

Dolphins in marine zoos have been observed inventing their own games. Bottlenosed dolphins often blow bubble rings in play, and lactating calves are quick to learn and demonstrate this behaviour. Orinoco River dolphins at

BELOW: Grey whales may travel up to 20,000 km (12,400 miles) in order to calve in the safety of the shallow lagoons around Baja and California.

BELOW: Very little is known about the Atlantic spotted dolphin, found off the south-east coast of the USA. The markings of the juvenile (below) make it easily distinguishable from the adult of the species (above).

Duisberg Zoological Gardens (FRG) will create large bubble rings and then swim through them, as well as play with a wide range of objects presented to them. A female bottlenosed dolphin at the Brighton Dolphinarium has been observed chasing the other pool residents with seaweed. Play behaviour in cetaceans probably developed from the intense curiosity that they show towards new things.

Whether play, or the other social behaviours described, are a sign of high intelligence is impossible to say.

Cetaceans were once thought to be our intellectual equals – however, recent research seems to indicate that they may not be as intelligent as was first thought. Although cetaceans may live in a social unit, the male seems to play little or no part in the rearing of the young. The cetacean brain is large and convoluted and has a ratio of brain to body size almost equal to our own. This was one of the main features that led scientists to believe that dolphins were highly intelligent animals capable of abstract thought. Their big brains are now con-

RIGHT: Pilot whales are highly social animals, who often congregate in large groups, sometimes numbering several hundred. This female and calf are in the Pacific Ocean, off Hawaii.

sidered to be necessary to process and store the large quantities of incoming sound information. However, cetaceans have evolved in a very different environment from our own, and so it may be wrong to measure their intelligence in the same way that we measure our own. Even if cetaceans do not turn out to be as super-intelligent as we once thought, there is still no reason for us not to admire and respect them.

BELOW: Dolphins seem to enjoy leaping and cavorting at sea, a behaviour often observed in friendly dolphins when in human company.

LIVING IN
A WORLD
OF SOUND

LEFT: A group of
common dolphins is
seen porpoising
quite close to shore.

The sea was once thought to be a silent world, whose inhabitants were believed to make little or no noise. We are now able to scan the seas with high-tech apparatus, and have discovered it to be a world of sound where fish, mammals and invertebrates communicate using a variety of thrums, snaps and clicks. Whales and dolphins are the most adept of all the marine inhabitants at using sound. They live in a three-dimensional world where visibility is very poor and produce sounds to orientate themselves and communicate within their environment. We, on the other hand, live in a world of light and colour and perceive our world through sight. In this way at least, humans and cetaceans differ greatly. Whales and dolphins produce a wide range of sounds, some of which are social calls and others which are navigational. Sound travels four and a half times faster underwater than it does in air, making it a very effective form of communication.

Killer whales (*Orcinus orca*) are extremely vocal and use a wide range of social calls to help strengthen the bond between pod members. Each pod has its own readily identifiable calls which are produced by all members of that pod. Some pods are easily distinguished while othes produce calls that are more similar. The latter groups may have been related at one time and so carry part of the original call. Some of the social calls serve to keep the pod members in constant contact, particularly when feeding, as they may become scattered over a wide area during the excitement of the hunt.

One of the most fascinating uses of sound by cetaceans is their ability to echolocate. By producing high-frequency sounds and listening for their returning echoes, they are able to build up a 'sound picture' of their immediate environment, helping them to navigate and detect their prey. Not all cetaceans are thought to possess this ability, but much study has been done regarding the echolocation abilities of the bottle-nosed dolphin *(Tursiops truncatus)*. Studies on this species have shown them to have a very effective sonar system,

RIGHT: A bottlenosed dolphin investigates a toy using sonar.

Melon focuses
sound

Lower jaw

The role of echolocation in cetacean communication is still not
fully understood, but researchers agree that it provides a very
sophisticated navigational sense. Echolocation is used for
direction-finding location sensing at long range, and also at
short range (using high-frequency signals) to determine the
texture and internal structure of objects. With echolocation, a
dolphin can determine water depth, distinguish a predator
from likely prey and judge the nature of nearby coastal
features.

Transmitted sound

Returning echo

echoes that are stored in the dolphin's memory. Dolphins often use their echolocation systems to investigate objects at close proximity. This may in part be due to the visual blind spot directly in front of them.

Cetaceans have no vocal cords – instead, the sounds are produced in the larynx and blowhole region with the aid of muscular action. The high-pitched sounds used for echolocation may be focused by the pad of fatty tissue known as the melon, situated in the forehead, which is thought to act as an acoustical lens (the melon distinguishes toothed from baleen whales as only the former have it). The sound travels through the water and bounces back from anything within range, returning to the cetacean as an echo. Until recently, it was thought that sounds picked up by the bottlenosed dolphin's lower jaw were transmitted to the inner ear via a fat-filled cavity. Recent research, however, suggests that the high-frequency sounds used in echolocation are in fact detected and received via the dolphin's teeth, which travel to the brain via nerves.

As well as using echolocation to detect prey, killer whales also spy-hop – that is, thrusting their upper bodies out of the water to look for signs of distant fish schools. When hunting other mammals such as seals, the killer whales are silent, as their calls would soon alert the seals to their presence.

Although cetaceans use sound to a high degree, most cetaceans have fairly good eyesight, both above and below the water. The beluga whale uses both sight and sound to locate its prey, which often includes crustaceans and marine

more efficient than the apparatus used in submarines, and very sensitive hearing. Bottlenosed dolphins are not just able to determine shape, size and distance using sound, but can also visualize internal structure. This may be used to recognize fish prey, as each individual fish will reflect a different echo, depending on the size of the swim bladder. These echoes may then be matched with

OPPOSITE:
Much of the
knowledge that we
have obtained
regarding the beluga
whale has come
from studies on
animals in marine
parks. This elusive
'white whale' is
found in waters
around northern
USSR, North
America and
Greenland.

worms as well as schooling fish. The beluga whale is sometimes known as the sea canary due to its very audible repertoire of whistles, moos and chirps. Cetaceans usually vocalize underwater and it is only in marine zoos that they can be heard 'singing' in the air.

The sperm whale (*Physeter macro-cephalus*) is thought to be able to see for a distance of 30 m (100 ft), which is only two or three times its own body length. Sperm whales produce a wide variety of vocalizations and some scientists believe them to have echo-

location capabilities. Sperm whales, which dive to great depths for their prey, are thought to be able to stun their prey using pure sound.

To river dolphins, which live in muddy rivers and estuaries, echolocation is essential for orientation and location of prey, which consists mainly of fish and freshwater crustaceans. River dolphins are a rather primitive group of cetaceans that have retained some of the features present in the dolphins' early ancestors. The river dolphin's eyes are very small and were once

BELOW: Recent
research suggests
that the 88 pointed
teeth of the
bottlenosed dolphin
act as sound
receptors to assist in
their excellent
echolocation
capabilities.

ABOVE: The sperm whale is easily recognized by its huge head and shorter lower jaw. These whales can dive to great depths where they are able to scan the darkness for squid using echolocation.

thought to be non-functional. Studies on the Indus River dolphin (*Platanista minor*), however, suggest that they do have some vision above water.

The most musical of all the cetaceans is the humpback whale (*Megaptera novaeangliae*), the only animal which can boast to having had a top-selling single in the charts, when, in 1970, their eerie and haunting but beautiful sounds were heard by many people for the first time. Scientific studies on humpback whale sounds have revealed them to be true songs, containing an ordered sequence of units similar to those of song birds. Although the exact function of the song is unclear, it is thought to have some sexual meaning.

Humpback whales do not sing all the year round and singing is confined almost entirely to the winter breeding grounds. The singing whales are thought to be solitary males, possibly announcing their sexual condition. The males start to sing as soon as they reach the breeding grounds. The song itself may last up to 35 minutes, with a definite beginning and a definite end. If a whale is interrupted mid-song, it will recommence exactly where it left off. Small groups of males may build up around a female who may or may not have a calf. Only one male escorts the female at one time, but this position may change throughout the day. When a male joins the group, it stops singing and only recommences when it leaves the group.

All the whales within one region sing the same song; however, individual whales seem to possess a personal characteristic to their voice, so keeping their own identity. This characteristic may allow females to recognize specific males. The content of the song will slowly change over several seasons.

Cetaceans are also thought to communicate in other ways. Jaw clapping is used as a warning by older toothed whales and has been recorded in the bottlenosed dolphin.

Another behaviour noted in many cetaceans, including killer whales, sperm whales and right whales (*Eubalaena glacialis*), is 'lobtailing'. The whale hangs head down in the water with its tail flukes in the air. The whale swings its tail to and fro several times before bringing it down on the water with a mighty slap which can be heard for miles around. Lobtailing may be a threatening behaviour or a social communication. Many whale species

BELOW: Humpback whale in its winter breeding grounds in Hawaiian waters. Few sights are more awe-inspiring than the aerial acrobatics of the humpback whale yet sadly, this spectacle may disappear forever, as the humpback whale faces extinction.

have been observed lobtailing in stormy seas and it may be used as a form of communication when normal sound contact is limited.

One of the most dramatic behaviours displayed by whales is breaching, when a whale leaps into the air, twists its body and crashes down into the water on its back. The most spectacular breaching behaviour is demonstrated by the humpback whale, whose aerial acrobatics are a beautiful and awesome sight to witness. Again, the exact function of breaching is not clear, but suggested possibilities include the dislodging of parasites; advertising the whale's location; or that it is part of some form of sexual ritual. Breaching may also be performed just for the sheer enjoyment of it.

Breaching is similar to porpoising, a behaviour displayed in dolphins and porpoises, including Commerson's dolphin *(Cephalorhynchus commersonii)* and the common dolphin *(Delphinus delphis)*. These small cetaceans porpoise to reduce friction on their bodies when surfacing to breathe, which helps to conserve energy, particularly during long migrations. Spinner dolphins *(Stenella longirostris)* are also very acrobatic and can be seen spinning on their longitudinal axes as they leap high into the air. Dusky dolphins *(Lagenorhynchus obscurus)* too make acrobatic leaps which seem to have no function other than play.

Cetaceans also use body language, a typical example of this being the S-shaped position adopted by male bottle-

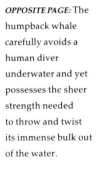

OPPOSITE PAGE: The humpback whale carefully avoids a human diver underwater and yet possesses the sheer strength needed to throw and twist its immense bulk out of the water.

BELOW: The common dolphin is just one of many species known to *porpoise,* a behaviour designed to conserve the dolphin's energy while travelling over long distances.

nosed dolphins prior to mating. Touch is also an important sense for dolphins. It is not only used in a social context, but also to investigate objects following a preliminary sonar investigation. Human infants use touch to explore their surroundings, but as we grow up, touch is used to a far lesser degree.

It has always been our dream to be able to talk to animals, which in turn has led us to view many of the higher animals through anthropomorphic eyes. However, serious research has suggested that some form of two-way communication may one day be possible. If such communication is to come about, we will have to use a 'language' that is common to both participants. Research with Koko, a female gorilla, showed the possibility of two-way communication using sign language. Koko not only mastered the language,

but also demonstrated many human attributes such as joking, teasing and insulting. The study revealed some very exciting results and although they have been criticized, they are still very encouraging.

Studies with a female killer whale named Gudrun indicated that two-way communication may be possible with some cetaceans. The researchers produced stylized replica sounds based on previous vocalizations recorded from Gudrun. The sounds were given meaning: 'take', 'give or bring', 'dumb-bell', 'fender' and 'fish'. Gudrun was found to be capable of producing the action and object sounds in a meaningful order (for example, 'give dumb-bell'), and correct results were achieved at a rate of 95%. Again, more research needs to be done in this area, but the results are certainly promising.

ABOVE: Many species of dolphin possess a natural camouflage called counter shading. The darker upper surface of the dolphin's body acts as a camouflage when seen from above and the lighter underside acts as a camouflage when seen from below.

FOUR

IDENTIFYING WHALES AND DOLPHINS AT SEA

LEFT: The unique
spinning acrobatics
of the spinner
dolphin make it
instantly
recognizable.
Spinner dolphins are
found in most
tropical waters.

The privileged few who have seen whales and dolphins in the wild usually have to be content with a quick glimpse of a fin, tail fluke or spout, before it disappears beneath the waves. Whales and dolphins are difficult to spot at the best of times, and even harder to identify. However, with the help of a guidebook to cetaceans, a camera and a note pad to record observations, you may find the problem of identification much easier.

Before you start to look for whales and dolphins, it may be helpful to refer to your guidebook and find out what species you may expect to see in your area. Some species are easier to identify than others. The male narwhal (*Mono-*

ABOVE: A plate from *Giant Fishes, Whales and Dolphins* by J. R. Norman and F. C. Fraser, published in 1937, exemplifying the diverse forms of cetaceans.

LEFT: Blue whales can be identified by their blue mottled colouring and the small dorsal fin placed far back on the body.

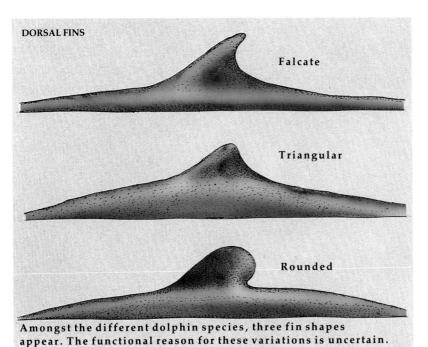

DORSAL FINS

Falcate

Triangular

Rounded

Amongst the different dolphin species, three fin shapes appear. The functional reason for these variations is uncertain.

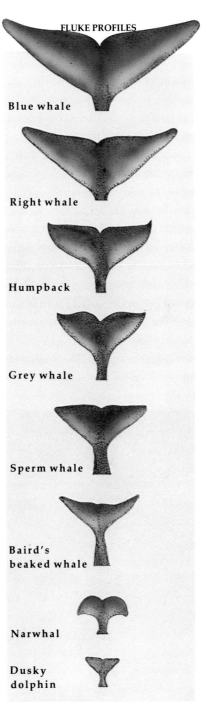

Blue whale

Right whale

Humpback

Grey whale

Sperm whale

Baird's beaked whale

Narwhal

Dusky dolphin

FLUKE PROFILES
Viewed from above, the fluke may vary considerably between whale species.

don monoceros), for instance, is easy to identify, as he possesses a long tusk which may reach a length of 2.7 m (8.8 ft). The function of the tusk is not known, but it may be used to help assert his dominance during the breeding season. The tusk from dead narwhals is occasionally washed ashore, and this may have been instrumental in creating the legend of the unicorn.

Whales also have other characteristics which may aid identification. For example, not all species of cetacean have a dorsal fin. Some species, such as the sperm whale (*Physeter macrocephalus*), bowhead whale (*Balaena mysticetus*) and the finless porpoise (*Neophocaena phocaenoides*) have no dorsal fin, although the sperm whale does have a dermal ridge. Humpback whales (*Megaptera novaeangliae*) have very long white pectoral fins which make this species easily identifiable underwater, or when breaching.

Natural markings and features may also be used to aid identification. Killer whales (*Orcinus orca*) can be identified by their black-and-white markings and tall, upright dorsal fins. The pilot whale (*Globicephala*) is black and has no beak, while the beluga whale (*Delphinapterus leucas*) is white. The northern bottlenosed whale (*Hyperoodon ampullatus*) has a massive forehead. Some species of dolphin, such as the common dolphin (*Delphinus delphis*) and the spinner dolphin (*Stenella longirostiris*) can be distinguished from other species by their long beaks.

Scientists studying whale and dolphin populations have been able to use natural markings to identify individual whales. Nicks on the edge of the killer whale's dorsal fin can be used to recognize individual animals, as can the outline of the grey saddle-shaped mark behind the dorsal fin. The northern right whale (*Eubalaena glacialis*) has encrustations on its head and jaw, the pattern being unique in each individual. The markings on the underside of the humpback whale's tail can also be used to identify individual animals, as can the scars and encrustations on the grey whale (*Eschrichtius robustus*).

Many whales, particularly the slower baleen whales, are host to barnacles, some of which are species-specific – that is, they are found only on one species of whale. Whales and dolphins are also host to a wide range of parasites, some of which burrow into their skin, while others, such as the whale louse, live on the surface, often in the wart-like callosities on the head of some baleen whales.

The subfamily Ziphiidae contains 18 species of beaked whale, some of which

ABOVE: The right whale's head has wart-like callosites, which form unique patterns, making it possible to identify individual whales. The right whale was the favorite target of whalers as it has a high oil yield and floated when it was killed, making it the ideal species to hunt.

LEFT: The markings on the underside of the humpback whale's tail are unique to each animal, making it possible to study their migration and social structure.

are thought to be very rare. One species, Longman's beaked whale (*Mesoplodon pacificus*), has never been seen in the flesh and is only known from two skulls that were washed ashore. Shepherd's beaked whale (*Tasmacetus shepherdi*) has only been observed on a few occasions. Many male beaked whales bear a pair of enlarged teeth which grow from the lower jaw, which look rather like fangs. Beaked whales are thought to feed mainly on squid, although not much is known about the biology and natural history of these animals.

Another group of cetaceans is the river dolphin family (Platanistidae), which lives almost entirely in fresh water. Most species are similar in appearance and have a long, narrow beak which resembles that of the fish-eating gavial of the crocodile family. Fresh-water dolphins differ from other marine species of dolphin by having a short neck and broad pectoral fins. They are thought to be a rather primitive group of cetaceans.

Observing behavioural displays may also give a clue to identifying the species. Bottlenosed dolphins (*Tursiops truncatus*), common dolphins (*Delphinus delphis*) and dusky dolphins (*Lagenorhynchus obscurus*) are all known to bow ride. Breaching is demonstrated by grey whales, humpback whales and killer whales, which also gives a clear view of the animal's features. Other behaviours which may aid identification include lobtailing and spy-hopping. Killer whales, sperm whales and right whales all exhibit lobtailing, while killer whales, pilot whales (*Globicephala*) and grey whales spy-hop to look for signs of distant prey, to get their bear-

ABOVE: The rough-toothed dolphin is found in most tropical and sub-tropical waters. Rough-toothed dolphins are also attracted by ships and love to ride the bow waves. They can usually be identified by their sloping forehead which continues to the end of its long slender beak.

LEFT: Grey whales are one of several species of cetacean known to spy-hop, raising their heads out of the water to survey their surroundings.

IDENTIFYING WHALES AND DOLPHINS AT SEA

55

ings or look out for predators. The twisting acrobatics of the spinner dolphin are unmistakable.

Many of the large whales can be identified by their spout and diving sequence. The spout is formed by water vapour, which is exhaled by a whale as it comes to the surface. The vapour then condenses to form a large cloud which can be seen from a great distance. It has been estimated that the air exhaled from the lungs of a humpback whale travels at about 480 kph (300 mph). The shape of the spout depends on the size and shape of the blowhole, or blowholes, as some species have two. Early whalers were able to detect the presence of whales by their spout or blow. Upon sighting whales, the lookout would shout down 'There she blows!' and the hunt would commence. The sperm whale's blowhole is situated on the tip of the head causing the spout to angle forwards. The right whale has two blowholes, thus producing a double spout, and the fin whale (*Balaenoptera physalus*) produces a tall, thin spout (*see diagram*). Whales can also be identified by their diving sequence. For instance, the sei whale (*Balaenoptera borealis*), Bryde's whale (*Balaenoptera edeni*) and fin whale do not lift their tail flukes out of the water when diving, whereas most other species do. By comparing observations such as the shape of the spout, diving sequence, natural markings and behavioural patterns, it should be possible to identify the species with the aid of a guidebook.

There are many cetacean groups and societies throughout the world who welcome information on cetacean sightings and may produce identification charts to ensure that data recorded are consistent for all sightings

BELOW: The encrustations, mottled markings and shape of the spout identify this whale as a grey whale. As their migration brings them close to land, they are the species of whale most likely to be seen from the shore.

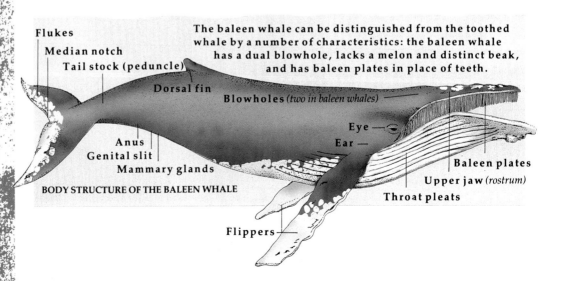

The baleen whale can be distinguished from the toothed whale by a number of characteristics: the baleen whale has a dual blowhole, lacks a melon and distinct beak, and has baleen plates in place of teeth.

Flukes
Median notch
Tail stock (peduncle)
Dorsal fin
Blowholes (*two in baleen whales*)
Eye
Ear
Anus
Genital slit
Mammary glands
Baleen plates
Upper jaw (*rostrum*)
Throat pleats
BODY STRUCTURE OF THE BALEEN WHALE
Flippers

DIVING SEQUENCE OF WHALES

A and B show a humpback whale; C and D depict a right whale.

IDENTIFYING WHALES BY SPOUT SHAPE

A Right whale   C Humpback whale
B Fin whale   D Sperm whale

One of the main problems with conserving cetaceans is that not enough is known about the populations of many species. Where a species is thought to be threatened by human impact on the environment, often there is not enough information available on previous populations with which present stocks can be compared. Thus it is difficult to assess the problem. Many organizations actively encourage the general public to take part in cetacean surveys. This type of 'practical conservation' can provide important information for the future and is very rewarding for the participant. It often stimulates people to become increasingly involved in voluntary conservation work.

SPECIES LIST

The following species list represents all of the 78 known species of cetacean. To ensure that this list is as complete as possible, the weights and lengths of some species are given as averages, while others are shown as maxima. For 37 out of the 78 species, an accurate weight is not known, so their weights have not been included. On the whole, the larger cetaceans can only be studied at sea, and it is only through whaling records and strandings that details of some species are known.

• Recorded information on many species is incomplete. The weight of the pygmy right whale (*Capanea marginata*), for example, is based on a single instance when the animal was weighed. Some species are rarely seen:

Blainville's beaked whale (*Mesoplodon densirostris*) has only been spotted on a few occasions, while Longman's beaked whale (*M. pacificus*) has only been identified from two skulls that were washed ashore. There are also two other species belonging to the beaked whale family (*Ziphiidae*) that have yet to be identified.

• Some species are known to be endangered, vulnerable or threatened according to IUCN Red Data Book categories. However, there are many species which are classified as being 'not threatened' whose status may well change in the near future. If this is thought likely, the status 'not threatened' is followed by a question mark.

• If nothing else, this species list reflects the problems of recording even basic information about such an elusive group of aquatic mammals.

WHALE AND DOLPHIN SPECIES LIST

List includes: name, Latin name, length, weight and status.

★★★*Note:* Status NT – 'not threatened'.
Status NT? – not classified as threatened, but may be in the future.
Status 'Not known' – insufficient information to determine status; may be endangered or vulnerable.

Some weights are average, while others are maximum. Where weight is not given, there are no positive records.

**SUPERFAMILY:
Platanistoidea**
FAMILY: **Platanistidae**
NAME: Ganges River dolphin
LATIN NAME: *Platanista
gangetica*
DISTRIBUTION: India,
Bangladesh, Nepal,
Bhutan
MAX LENGTH: 2.5 m (8.2 ft)
MAX WEIGHT: 84 kg (185 lb)
STATUS: Vulnerable

NAME: Indus River dolphin
LATIN NAME: *Platanista minor*
DISTRIBUTION: Pakistan
MAX LENGTH: 2.5 m (8.2 ft)
MAX WEIGHT: 84 kg (185 lb)
STATUS: Endangered

FAMILY: **Pontoporiidae
(Subfamily: Lipotinae)**
NAME: Yangtse River
dolphin
LATIN NAME: *Lipotes vexillifer*
DISTRIBUTION: China
MAX LENGTH: 2.5 m (8.2 ft)
MAX WEIGHT: 167 kg (368 lb)
STATUS: Endangered

**(Subfamily:
Pontoporiinae)**
NAME: La Plata dolphin
LATIN NAME: *Pontoporia
blainvillei*
DISTRIBUTION: Brazil,
Uruguay, Argentina
MAX LENGTH: 1.7 m (5.6 ft)
MAX WEIGHT: 52 kg (115 lb)
STATUS: Not known

FAMILY: **Iniidae**
NAME: Amazon River dolphin
LATIN NAME: *Inia geoffrensis*
DISTRIBUTION: Brazil, Bolivia,
Peru, Ecuador, Colombia,
Venezuela, Guyana
MAX LENGTH: 2.5 m (8.5 ft)
MAX WEIGHT: 160 kg (353 lb)
STATUS: Vulnerable

**SUPERFAMILY:
Delphinvidea**
FAMILY: **Monodontidae
(Subfamily: Orcaellinae)**
NAME: Irrawaddy dolphin
LATIN NAME: *Orcaella
brevirostris*
DISTRIBUTION: Tropical Indo-
Pacific region (inshore
waters)
MAX LENGTH: 2.8 m (9.2 ft)
MAX WEIGHT: 190 kg (419 lb)
STATUS: Not known

**(Subfamily:
Delphinapterinae)**
NAME: Beluga whale
LATIN NAME: *Delphinapterus
leucas*
DISTRIBUTION: N USSR,
N America, Greenland
MAX LENGTH: 5.72 m (18.7 ft)
MAX WEIGHT: 1.6 tonnes (1.6
tons)
STATUS: Not known

**(Subfamily:
Monodontinae)**
NAME: Narwhal
LATIN NAME: *Monodon
monoceros*
DISTRIBUTION: N USSR,
N America, Greenland
MAX LENGTH: 4.7 m (15.4 ft);
tusk max 2.7 m (8.9 ft)
MAX WEIGHT: 1.6 tonnes (1.6
tons)
STATUS: Not known

FAMILY: **Phocoenidae
(Subfamily: Phocoeninae)**
NAME: Harbour porpoise
LATIN NAME: *Phocoena phocoena*
DISTRIBUTION: Arctic,
N Atlantic, N Pacific
Oceans, Black Sea
AVERAGE LENGTH: 2.0 m
(6.6 ft)
AVERAGE WEIGHT: 90 kg (198 lb)
STATUS: Not known

NAME: Burmeister's porpoise
LATIN NAME: *Phocoena
spinipinnis*
DISTRIBUTION: Seas off the
Falkland Islands,
southern S America – east
coast to Uruguay
AVERAGE LENGTH: 1.8 m (5.9 ft)
AVERAGE WEIGHT: ?
STATUS: NT?

NAME: Vaquita
LATIN NAME: *Phocoena sinus*
DISTRIBUTION: Gulf of California
AVERAGE LENGTH: 1.5 m (4.9 ft)
AVERAGE WEIGHT: 47 kg (104 lb)
STATUS: Vulnerable

NAME: Finless porpoise
LATIN NAME: *Neophocaena
phocaenoides*
DISTRIBUTION: Indo-Pacific
Ocean from Iran to New
Guinea and Japan
AVERAGE LENGTH: 1.9 m (6.2 ft)
AVERAGE WEIGHT: ?
STATUS: NT?

**(Subfamily:
Phocoenoides)**
NAME: Spectacled porpoise
LATIN NAME: *Australophocaena
dioptonca*
DISTRIBUTION: E coast of
S America, Falkland Islands
AVERAGE LENGTH: 2.2 m (7.2 ft)
AVERAGE WEIGHT: ?
STATUS: NT?

NAME: Dall's porpoise
LATIN NAME: *Phocoenoides dalli*
DISTRIBUTION: N Pacific Ocean
– becoming few, S Japan,
S California
AVERAGE LENGTH: 2.2 m (7.2 ft)
AVERAGE WEIGHT: 220 kg
(485 lb)
STATUS: NT?

FAMILY: **Delphinidae
(Subfamily: Steninae)**
NAME: Rough-toothed
dolphin
LATIN NAME: *Steno bredanensis*
DISTRIBUTION: Tropical and
subtropical waters
AVERAGE LENGTH: 2.8 m (9.2 ft)
AVERAGE WEIGHT: ?
STATUS: NT

NAME: Indo-Pacific
humpbacked dolphin
LATIN NAME: *Sousa chinensis*
DISTRIBUTION: Seas off S and E
Africa, Red Sea, Persian
Gulf, India, New Guinea,
N Australia, S China
AVERAGE LENGTH: 2.8 m (9.2 ft)
AVERAGE WEIGHT: 285 kg
(628 lb)
STATUS: NT?

NAME: Atlantic humpbacked
dolphin
LATIN NAME: *Sousa tenszii*
DISTRIBUTION: Coastal waters
of W Africa

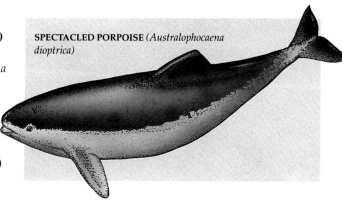

SPECTACLED PORPOISE (*Australophocaena
dioptrica*)

AVERAGE LENGTH: 2.8 m (9.2 ft)
AVERAGE WEIGHT: 285 kg
(628 lb)
STATUS: NT?

NAME: Tucuxi
LATIN NAME: *Sotalia fluviatilis*
DISTRIBUTION: Amazon River,
E coast of S America from
Rio de Janeiro to
Venezuela
AVERAGE LENGTH: 1.9 m (6.2 ft)
AVERAGE WEIGHT: ?
STATUS: NT?

(Subfamily: Delphininae)
NAME: White-beaked
dolphin
LATIN NAME: *Lagenorhynchus
albirostris*
DISTRIBUTION: N Atlantic
Ocean from New England
to Iceland and W Europe,
Greenland
AVERAGE LENGTH: 3.1 m (10.2 ft)
AVERAGE WEIGHT: ?
STATUS: NT

NAME: Dusky dolphin
LATIN NAME: *Lagenorhynchus
obscurus*
DISTRIBUTION: Seas off New
Zealand, southern
Australia, S America,
S Africa
AVERAGE LENGTH: 2.1 m (6.9 ft)
AVERAGE WEIGHT: ?
STATUS: NT?

NAME: Pacific white-sided
dolphin
LATIN NAME: *Lagenorhynchus
obliquidens*
DISTRIBUTION: Pacific waters of
Japan and S Alaska to
Baja, California
AVERAGE LENGTH: 2.3 m (7.5 ft)
AVERAGE WEIGHT: 150 kg
(331 lb)
STATUS: NT

NAME: Atlantic white-sided
dolphin
LATIN NAME: *Lagenorhynchus
acutus*
DISTRIBUTION: N Atlantic
AVERAGE LENGTH: 2.7 m (8.9 ft)
AVERAGE WEIGHT: ?
STATUS: NT

NAME: Peace's dolphin
LATIN NAME: *Lagenorhynchus
australis*
DISTRIBUTION: Southern
S America
AVERAGE LENGTH: 2.2 m (7.2 ft)
AVERAGE WEIGHT: ?
STATUS: NT?

NAME: Risso's dolphin
LATIN NAME: *Grampus griseus*
DISTRIBUTION: Most temperate
and tropical waters
AVERAGE LENGTH: 4.0 m (13.1 ft)
AVERAGE WEIGHT: ?
STATUS: NT

NAME: Hourglass dolphin
LATIN NAME: *Lagenorhynchus
cruciger*
DISTRIBUTION: Cold water of
the southern oceans
AVERAGE LENGTH: 1.8 m (6.0 ft)
AVERAGE WEIGHT: ?
STATUS: NT

NAME: Bottlenosed dolphin
LATIN NAME: *Tursiops truncatus*
DISTRIBUTION: Worldwide,
warm and temperate waters
AVERAGE LENGTH: 4.5 m (14.8 ft)
AVERAGE WEIGHT: 275 kg (606 lb)
STATUS: NT?

NAME: Atlantic spotted
dolphin
LATIN NAME: *Stenella frontalis*
DISTRIBUTION: SE coast of USA
AVERAGE LENGTH: 2.3 m (7.5 ft)
AVERAGE WEIGHT: ?
STATUS: NT

NAME: Pantropical spotted
dolphin
LATIN NAME: *Stenella attenuata*
DISTRIBUTION: All warm
waters
AVERAGE LENGTH: 2.2 m (7.2 ft)
AVERAGE WEIGHT: ?
STATUS: NT?

NAME: Spinner dolphin
LATIN NAME: *Stenella
longirostris*
DISTRIBUTION: Most tropical
waters
AVERAGE LENGTH: 2.2 m (7.2 ft)
AVERAGE WEIGHT: ?
STATUS: NT?

NAME: Clymene dolphin
LATIN NAME: *Stenella clymene*
DISTRIBUTION: Atlantic Ocean,
E coast of America,
W coast of Africa
AVERAGE LENGTH: 2.0 m (6.6 ft)
AVERAGE WEIGHT: ?
STATUS: NT

NAME: Striped dolphin
LATIN NAME: *Stenella
coeruleoalba*
DISTRIBUTION: Most warm and
temperate waters of the
world
AVERAGE LENGTH: 2.7 m (6.0 ft)
AVERAGE WEIGHT: ?
STATUS: NT?

NAME: Common dolphin
LATIN NAME: *Delphinus delphis*
DISTRIBUTION: Most warm and
temperate waters of the
world
AVERAGE LENGTH: 2.5 m (8.2 ft)
AVERAGE WEIGHT: 75 kg (165 lb)
STATUS: NT

**(Subfamily:
Lissodelphinae)**
NAME: Northern right whale
dolphin

LATIN NAME: *Lissodelphis
borealis*
DISTRIBUTION: N Pacific
temperate waters
AVERAGE LENGTH: 3.1 m (10.2 ft)
AVERAGE WEIGHT: ?
STATUS: NT

NAME: Southern right whale
dolphin
LATIN NAME: *Lissodelphis
peronii*
DISTRIBUTION: Southern
oceans
AVERAGE LENGTH: 2.4 m (7.9 ft)
AVERAGE WEIGHT: ?
STATUS: NT

**(Subfamily:
Cephalorhynchinae)**
NAME: Commerson's
dolphin
LATIN NAME: *Cephalorhynchus
commersonii*
DISTRIBUTION: Cool waters off
southern S America,
Falkland Islands
AVERAGE LENGTH: 1.3 m (4.3 ft)
AVERAGE WEIGHT: ?
STATUS: Not known

NAME: Black dolphin
LATIN NAME: *Cephalorhynchus
eutropia*
DISTRIBUTION: Coastal waters
of Chile
AVERAGE LENGTH: 1.7 m (5.6 ft)
AVERAGE WEIGHT: 63 kg
(139 lb)
STATUS: Not known

NAME: Heaviside's dolphin
LATIN NAME: *Cephalorhynchus
heavisidii*
DISTRIBUTION: Coastal waters
of southwestern Africa
AVERAGE LENGTH: 1.7 m (5.6 ft)
AVERAGE WEIGHT: 74 kg
(163 lb)
STATUS: Not known

NAME: Hector's dolphin
LATIN NAME: *Cephalorhynchus hectori*
DISTRIBUTION: Off SW Africa
AVERAGE LENGTH: 1.6 m (5.2 ft)
AVERAGE WEIGHT: 57 kg (126 lb)
STATUS: Not known

NAME: False killer whale
LATIN NAME: *Pseudorca crassidens*
DISTRIBUTION: Worldwide, warm and tropical waters
AVERAGE LENGTH: 6.1 m (20.0 ft)
AVERAGE WEIGHT: 1.4 tonnes (1.4 tons)
STATUS: NT

NAME: Short-finned pilot whale
LATIN NAME: *Globicephala macrorhynchus*
DISTRIBUTION: All temperate waters of Atlantic, Pacific and Indian Oceans
AVERAGE LENGTH: 5.4 m (17.7 ft)
AVERAGE WEIGHT: ?
STATUS: NT

NAME: Arnoux's beaked whale
LATIN NAME: *Berardius arnuxii*
DISTRIBUTION: Cold and temperate waters of southern oceans
AVERAGE LENGTH: 10.0 m (32.8 ft)
AVERAGE WEIGHT: ?
STATUS: NT

SUPERFAMILY: Ziphioidea
FAMILY: **Ziphiidae**
NAME: Shepherd's beaked whale
LATIN NAME: *Tasmacetus shepherdi*
DISTRIBUTION: Southern hemisphere – rarely seen
AVERAGE LENGTH: 6–7 m (20–23 ft)
AVERAGE WEIGHT: ?
STATUS: NT

NAME: Longman's beaked whale
LATIN NAME: *Mesoplodon pacificus*
DISTRIBUTION: Known only from two skulls found washed up off Australia and Somalia
AVERAGE LENGTH: ?
AVERAGE WEIGHT: ?
STATUS: NT

NAME: Sowerby's beaked whale
LATIN NAME: *Mesoplodon bidens*
DISTRIBUTION: N Atlantic
AVERAGE LENGTH: 5.0 m (16.4 ft)
AVERAGE WEIGHT: ?
STATUS: NT

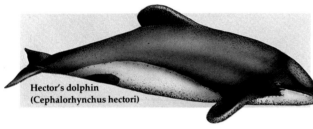

Hector's dolphin
(Cephalorhynchus hectori)

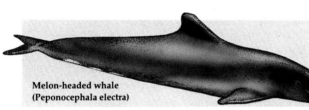

Melon-headed whale
(Peponocephala electra)

NAME: Melon-headed whale
LATIN NAME: *Peponocephala electra*
DISTRIBUTION: Warm and temperate waters of Atlantic and Pacific Oceans
AVERAGE LENGTH: 2.7 m (8.9 ft)
AVERAGE WEIGHT: ?
STATUS: NT

NAME: Pygmy killer whale
LATIN NAME: *Feresa attenuata*
DISTRIBUTION: Worldwide, warm and temperate waters
AVERAGE LENGTH: 2.7 m (8.9 ft)
AVERAGE WEIGHT: ?
STATUS: NT

NAME: Killer whale
LATIN NAME: *Orcinus orca*
DISTRIBUTION: Worldwide
AVERAGE LENGTH: 9.5 m (31.2 ft)
AVERAGE WEIGHT: 8.0 tonnes (8.0 tons)
STATUS: NT

NAME: Long-finned pilot whale
LATIN NAME: *Globicephala melaena*
DISTRIBUTION: Southern hemisphere, temperate waters of N Atlantic Ocean
AVERAGE LENGTH: 6.2 m (20.3 ft)
AVERAGE WEIGHT: 3.0 tonnes (3.0 tons)
STATUS: NT

NAME: Baird's beaked whale
LATIN NAME: *Berardiius bairdii*
DISTRIBUTION: Cold waters of N Pacific
MAX LENGTH: 12.8 m (42.0 ft)
MAX WEIGHT: 11.0 tonnes (10.8 tons)
STATUS: NT

NAME: Blainville's beaked whale
LATIN NAME: *Mesoplodon densirostris*
DISTRIBUTION: Rare species

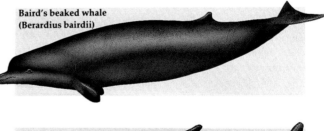

Baird's beaked whale
(Berardius bairdii)

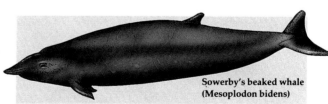

Sowerby's beaked whale
(Mesoplodon bidens)

spread throughout Atlantic and Pacific Oceans
AVERAGE LENGTH: 4.7 m (15.4 ft)
AVERAGE WEIGHT: ?
STATUS: NT

NAME: Gervais beaked whale
LATIN NAME: *Mesoplodon europeaeus*
DISTRIBUTION: Warm and temperate waters of the N Atlantic
AVERAGE LENGTH: 5.0 m (16.4 ft)
AVERAGE WEIGHT: ?
STATUS: NT

NAME: Strap-toothed whale
LATIN NAME: *Mesoplodon layardii*
DISTRIBUTION: Southern oceans
AVERAGE LENGTH: Just over 6.0 m (20.0 ft)
AVERAGE WEIGHT: ?
STATUS: NT

waters of southern hemisphere
AVERAGE LENGTH: 5.8 m (19.0 ft)
AVERAGE WEIGHT: ?
STATUS: NT

NAME: Stejneger's beaked whale
LATIN NAME: *Mesoplodon stejnegeri*
DISTRIBUTION: N Pacific
AVERAGE LENGTH: 5.3 m (17.4 ft)
AVERAGE WEIGHT: 1.5 tonnes (1.5 tons)
STATUS: NT

NAME: Andrew's beaked whale
LATIN NAME: *Mesoplodon bowdoini*
DISTRIBUTION: N Pacific
AVERAGE LENGTH: 4.6 m (15.1 ft)
AVERAGE WEIGHT: ?
STATUS: NT

NAME: True's beaked whale
LATIN NAME: *Mesoplodon mirus*
DISTRIBUTION: Mainly N Atlantic

NAME: Hubb's beaked whale
LATIN NAME: *Mesoplodon carlhubbsi*
DISTRIBUTION: Temperate waters of N Pacific
AVERAGE LENGTH: 5.3 m (17.4 ft)
AVERAGE WEIGHT: 1.5 tonnes (1.5 tons)
STATUS: NT

NAME: Southern bottlenosed whale
LATIN NAME: *Hyperoodon planifrons*
DISTRIBUTION: Temperate waters of the southern hemisphere
AVERAGE LENGTH: 7.5 m (24.6 ft)

Cuvier's beaked whale (Ziphius cavirostris)

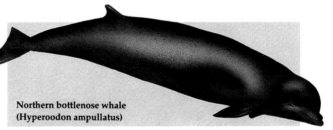
Northern bottlenose whale (Hyperoodon ampullatus)

Strap-toothed whale (Mesoplodon layardii)

NAME: Hector's beaked whale
LATIN NAME: *Mesoplodon hectori*
DISTRIBUTION: Temperate waters of southern hemisphere
AVERAGE LENGTH: 4.5 m (14.8 ft)
AVERAGE WEIGHT: ?
STATUS: NT

NAME: Gray's beaked whale
LATIN NAME: *Mesoplodon grayi*
DISTRIBUTION: Temperate

AVERAGE LENGTH: 5.3 m (17.4 ft)
AVERAGE WEIGHT: ?
STATUS: NT

NAME: Ginko-toothed beaked whale
LATIN NAME: *Mesoplodon ginkgodens*
DISTRIBUTION: Indo-Pacific Ocean, Japan to California
AVERAGE LENGTH: 5.0 m (16.4 ft)
AVERAGE WEIGHT: 1.5 tonnes (1.5 tons)
STATUS: NT

NAME: Cuvier's beaked whale
LATIN NAME: *Ziphius cavirostris*
DISTRIBUTION: Temperate and tropical waters
AVERAGE LENGTH: 6.9 m (22.6 ft)
AVERAGE WEIGHT: 2.9 tonnes (2.9 tons)
STATUS: NT

NAME: Northern bottlenosed whale
LATIN NAME: *Hyperoodon ampullatus*
DISTRIBUTION: N Atlantic Ocean
AVERAGE LENGTH: 9.8 m (32.2 ft)
AVERAGE WEIGHT: Several tonnes
STATUS: Not known

AVERAGE WEIGHT: Several tonnes
STATUS: NT

There are also thought to be two as yet unidentified species in the family **Ziphiidae**:
NAME: ?
LATIN NAME: *Mesoplodon* sp.
DISTRIBUTION: ?
AVERAGE LENGTH: ?
AVERAGE WEIGHT: ?
STATUS: ?

NAME: ?
LATIN NAME: *Hyperoodon* sp.
DISTRIBUTION: ?
AVERAGE LENGTH: ?
AVERAGE WEIGHT: ?
STATUS: ?

Bowhead (Balaena mysticetus)

Pygmy right whale
(Caperea marginata)

**SUPERFAMILY:
Physeteroidae**
FAMILY: **Physeteridae
(Subfamily: Physeterinae)**
NAME: Sperm whale
LATIN NAME: *Physeter
macrocephalus*
DISTRIBUTION: Worldwide
MAX LENGTH: Male – 18.3 m
(60.0 ft)
Female – 12.5 m (41.0 ft)
AVERAGE WEIGHT: Male – 57.1
tonnes (56.2 tons)
Female – 24.0 tonnes (23.6
tons)
STATUS: NT

FAMILY: **Kogiidae**
NAME: Pygmy sperm whale
LATIN NAME: *Kogia breviceps*
DISTRIBUTION: Worldwide,
tropical and warm waters
AVERAGE LENGTH: 3.4 m (11.2 ft)
MAX WEIGHT: 417 kg (919 lb)
STATUS: ?

NAME: Dwarf sperm whale
LATIN NAME: *Kogia simus*
DISTRIBUTION: Warm and
tropical waters
AVERAGE LENGTH: 2.7 m (8.9 ft)
AVERAGE WEIGHT: 272 kg
(600 lb)
STATUS: NT

SUBORDER: **Mysticeti (baleen
whales)**
FAMILY: **Balaenidae**
NAME: Bowhead whale
LATIN NAME: *Balaena
mysticetus*
DISTRIBUTION: Arctic,
N Atlantic, N Pacific Oceans
AVERAGE LENGTH: 20.0 m (65.6 ft)
AVERAGE WEIGHT: 107 tonnes
(105 tons)
STATUS: Endangered

NAME: Northern right
whale
LATIN NAME: *Eubalaena glacialis*
DISTRIBUTION: N Atlantic,
N Pacific Oceans
AVERAGE LENGTH: 18.0 m (59.1 ft)
AVERAGE WEIGHT: 109 tonnes
(107 tons)
STATUS: Endangered

NAME: Southern right
whale
LATIN NAME: *Eubalaena
australis*
DISTRIBUTION: S Atlantic,
Pacific, Indian, Southern
Oceans
AVERAGE LENGTH: 18.0 m (59.1 ft)
AVERAGE WEIGHT: 109 tonnes
(107 tons)
STATUS: Vulnerable

FAMILY: **Neobalaenidae**
NAME: Pygmy right whale
LATIN NAME: *Capanea
marginata*
DISTRIBUTION: Southern
temperate waters
AVERAGE LENGTH: 6.5 m (21.3 ft)
AVERAGE WEIGHT: 3.2 tonnes
(3.1 tons)
STATUS: NT

FAMILY: **Eschrichtiidae**
NAME: Grey whale
LATIN NAME: *Eschrichtius
robustus*
DISTRIBUTION: N Pacific
Ocean, Bering Sea
AVERAGE LENGTH: 14.6 m (47.9 ft)
AVERAGE WEIGHT: 34.4 tonnes
(33.9 tons)
STATUS: NT?

FAMILY: **Balaenopteridae
(Subfamily:
Balaenopterinae)**
NAME: Minke whale
LATIN NAME: *Balaenoptera
acutorostrata*
DISTRIBUTION: Cold and
temperate waters
AVERAGE LENGTH: 11.1 m (36.4 ft)
AVERAGE WEIGHT: 9.0 tonnes
(8.9 tons)
STATUS: NT

NAME: Sei whale
LATIN NAME: *Balaenoptera
borealis*
DISTRIBUTION: All oceans
AVERAGE LENGTH: 20.0 m
(65.6 ft)
AVERAGE WEIGHT: 38.4 tonnes
(37.8 tons)
STATUS: NT

NAME: Bryde's whale
LATIN NAME: *Balaenoptera edeni*
DISTRIBUTION: Tropical and
temperate waters of
Atlantic, Indian, W Pacific
Oceans
AVERAGE LENGTH: 15.5 m (50.9 ft)
AVERAGE LENGTH: 16.4 tonnes
(16.1 tons)
STATUS: NT

NAME: Blue whale
LATIN NAME: *Balaenoptera
musculus*
DISTRIBUTION: All oceans
AVERAGE LENGTH: 33.6 m
(110.2 ft)
AVERAGE WEIGHT: 193 tonnes
(190 tons)
STATUS: Vulnerable

NAME: Fin whale
LATIN NAME: *Balaenoptera
physalus*
DISTRIBUTION: All oceans
AVERAGE LENGTH:
N hemisphere – 24.0 m
(78.7 ft)
S hemisphere – 26.8 m
(87.9 ft)
AVERAGE WEIGHT: 70.7 tonnes
(69.5 tons)
STATUS: Vulnerable

**(Subfamily:
Megapterinae)**
NAME: Humpback whale
LATIN NAME: *Megaptera
novaeangliae*
DISTRIBUTION: All oceans
AVERAGE LENGTH: 18.0 m (59.1 ft)
AVERAGE WEIGHT: 41.5 tonnes
(40.8 tons)
STATUS: Vulnerable

FIVE

—

STRANDINGS

LEFT: Common
dolphins *(Delphinus
delphis)* swimming in
the Mediterranean
Sea, near Gibraltar.

Live cetacean strandings have intrigued scientists for many years. Many theories have been put forward to explain this phenomenon and it now seems likely that the various cases of stranding are caused by different factors.

One theory put forward is the one of disease. Disease or sickness caused by an internal or external parasite could cause a whale or dolphin to strand. Some mass strandings have occurred when the leading animal is so affected that it leads the other pod members into shallow water. Even though the rest of the pod could swim to safety, they remain with the leader and become stranded at low tide. Pilot whales (*Globicephala*) are often involved in mass strandings.

Another theory involves sloping beaches and open-ocean toothed whales which may become stranded in shallow water while following their prey. Toothed whales hunt using echolocation, and a gently sloping beach would not return an echo, so the animal may not be aware of the danger until it is too late. While this explanation may seem plausible in many cases, it does not account for those strandings which happen elsewhere. Only two-thirds of UK strandings occur on sloping beaches.

Another alternative is the geomagnetic theory. It is thought that whales and dolphins navigate by following the geomagnetic topography of the Earth, travelling parallel to the geomagnetic contours. These contours do not run in straight lines, but form hills, valleys and plains. In the featureless, open ocean, these contours provide whales

LEFT: One of the biggest mysteries surrounding cetaceans is the phenomenon of whale strandings. The cause of most strandings, such as this one involving pilot whales in the Orkney Islands in May 1983, are hard to discover.

Balæna. magna 60. perticas longa. 41. alta.

and dolphins with pathways to follow, but because the geomagnetic field fluctuates throughout the day, cetaceans have to learn these geomagnetic routes. This would be a very useful method of navigation in open water, but because there is no indication of where the contours intersect land, open-ocean species which have strayed off-course may become stranded. Coastal species may also make mistakes when navigating or misread the information due to disturbances in the geomagnetic field.

Studies of all UK live-stranding sites have shown them to be areas where geomagnetic contours are perpendicular to land from the sea, which supports the theory that live strandings are caused in the above manner. Areas where dead whales have been washed ashore have geomagnetic contours which are both parallel and perpendicular to the shore. Studies of other stranding sites so far support the geomagnetic theory.

Although there are about 16 different species of whale and dolphin that frequent British waters, over the last 70 years since records have been kept, there have only been 136 live strandings (minimum estimate) and 968 dead strandings (minimum estimate) recorded in British waters. Species most frequently involved in UK live strandings are the long-finned pilot whale (*Globicephala melaena*), the common

ABOVE: From *Theatrum Universale Omnium Animalium*, published in 1718.

DOLPHINS
AND WHALES

68

dolphin (*Delphinus delphis*) and the common porpoise (*Phocoena phocoena*), followed by the northern bottlenosed whale (*Hyperoodon ampullatus*). The species most commonly involved in dead strandings are the common porpoise, long-finned pilot whale and the common dolphin.

In England, Wales, Scotland and Northern Ireland, whales, dolphins and porpoises (along with sturgeon fish) are 'royal fish' and are the property of the Crown. Any strandings, dead or alive, must be reported to the receiver of wrecks. In the US, cetacean strandings come under the jurisdiction of the National Marine Fisheries Service.

If you do come across a stranded whale or dolphin, there are several things that you can do. Firstly, determine if the whale or dolphin is alive. Just because it is not moving, does not mean that it is dead. The best way to determine this is to check the blowhole to see if it is breathing. Stranded cetaceans usually beach laying on one side, which makes it easier to observe breathing. The normal relaxed position for the blowhole is closed and when the animal breathes, it will exhale first, then inhale very quickly.

Small cetaceans should take a breath every 20–60 seconds. However, a larger whale such as a baleen whale may breathe only once every 10–20 minutes. If the animal is dead, it may already be

BELOW: Some species of dolphin, such as Risso's dolphin, are solitary by nature, which may explain why some species are stranded in large numbers, while others are involved in single strandings.

BELOW: Pilot whales are the species most commonly involved in mass strandings. On some occasions they are successfully returned to the sea, while on others, the whales turn around and beach themselves a little further up the coast.
FAR RIGHT: Without the support of water the weight of the whale's body may damage vital internal organs.

partly decomposed. If the animal is alive, its body must be kept wet, or its delicate skin will dry out and crack. Wet towels or wet seaweed will do. Do not cover its blowhole and do not allow water to enter it.

If you are on your own, go for help by contacting either the coastguard or the police. Dolphinaria and museums are often helpful and may give advice, or if near enough may come to help. Dolphinaria may have equipment that can be used to help refloat the animal or may have facilities to temporarily house it if necessary. Do not attempt to drag the animal to the sea. If the animal is on its side, try to turn it upright as lung congestion may occur.

Should a large number of onlookers gather around, keep them back so as

not to cause the animal unnecessary distress. If the animal can be refloated and is of a size to be moved, then it can be gently rolled on to a sheet and dragged down to the water. If it is a large species, then a mobile crane and stretcher may be needed. In the case of a mass stranding, only the fittest animals are likely to survive. Any mothers and calves should be given priority treatment.

Dead animals also have to be reported and arrangements made to remove the body. Dead specimens are very useful to scientists or museums, who may take tissue samples for further study, and use the skeleton for scientific or educational purposes. If it is a toothed whale, they may be able to age the specimen by removing a tooth and cutting a cross-section to reveal growth rings of dentine, similar to the growth rings of a tree. Information such as the animal's size, weight and characteristics, and where it was stranded, should be sent (in the UK) to the British Museum of Natural History in London. In the US, information should be sent to the National Marine Fisheries Service, who will pass reports on to the Mammal Events Program at the Smithsonian Institute in Washington D.C.

LEFT: On occasions when a dead whale or dolphin is washed ashore, scientists have the ideal opportunity to collect data and specimens, like this humpback whale vertebrae, that can then be used for research or educational purposes.

FRIENDLY
ENCOUNTER

LEFT: Not all
dolphin encounters
are with solitary
animals. Some
human/dolphin
interactions involve
several dolphins, as
with these spotted
dolphins off the
Bahamas.

ABOVE: The most common species of dolphin involved with 'friendly encounters' is the bottlenosed dolphin. These dolphins actively seek out human company, for reasons known only to them.

Encounters between humans and cetaceans have been recorded all over the world. The animals involved in these encounters have become known as 'friendlies' because of their eagerness for cetacean/human interaction.

One of the best-known of these encounters involved a female bottlenosed dolphin (*Tursiops truncatus*) called Opo (short for Opononi) who interacted with swimmers and boats at Opononi in New Zealand during 1955. As with many friendly dolphin encounters, it was with children that Opo seemed to show most affinity. Opo did not allow physical contact straight away, and it was only after a series of encounters that Opo

allowed people to touch her. This is true of most other dolphin encounters of this kind. Opo, like all other friendly dolphins, was soon loved by almost everyone. However, some local fishermen resented the presence of dolphins, believing them to be responsible for scaring fish away and raiding their nets.

Off the coast of Florida in 1965, a friendly male bottlenosed dolphin called Nudge arrived on the scene. Nudge received his name because of his habit of nudging boats with his beak. Donald was another male bottlenosed dolphin who appeared along the west coast of the British Isles in 1972. Donald not only interacted with swimmers and divers but also showed great interest in boats, chains, marker buoys and other maritime objects. Donald also frequently manoeuvred moored boats and, like other dolphins, was attracted by the engine sounds from small boats. Although Donald took freshly caught fish offered to him by fishermen, they were later found discarded on the sea bed. The fish were probably taken to be used as a toy. Opo also refused fish offered to her.

Attempts were made to include Donald in a game with a beach ball and although he looked on inquisitively, he showed no interest in joining in. Opo, on the other hand, played frequently with a ball. Many of the friendly dolphins seem to have a preference for the

ABOVE: Spotted dolphins allowing a human diver to swim along with them. These dolphins could easily out-distance the diver if such attention was unwanted.

LEFT: The fact that some friendly dolphins in the wild seem familiar with toys, in this case a ball, has given rise to the idea that they may once have been residents of a coastal marine park.

colours yellow and orange, and objects which are so-coloured seem to receive a much closer inspection.

Both Donald and Opo would give people a ride on their backs (often children) or tow them along as they hung on to their dorsal fins. Bottlenosed dolphins in marine zoos often give their keepers similar rides. It is always the dolphin that initiates play and the encounter remains under the animal's control. The session ends when the dolphin decides it has had enough. Divers working in local waters are sometimes involved in chance encounters. On occasions, when a diver has finished working, the dolphin, who has not yet tired of the game, attempts to prevent the diver from leaving by nipping his flippers and prodding his equipment. If this behaviour does not

deliver the desired result, the dolphin may resort to pinning the diver to the sea bottom for several seconds. Dolphins and killer whales (*Orcinus orca*) in marine zoos may also try to prevent their trainer from leaving the pool during a play session.

Simo was a young male bottlenosed dolphin seen along the Welsh coast of the UK in 1984. Simo showed the same curiosity demonstrated during other friendly dolphin encounters. He was recorded interacting with a resident group of grey seals (*Halichoerus grypus*), and appeared to be actually playing with some of the younger ones.

In a remote corner of western Australia at a place called Monkey Mia, people and dolphins frequently meet. The dolphins arrive at a shallow lagoon in the early morning. People come from

ABOVE: Friendly dolphins are often attracted by the sound of small vessels and love to swim at high speed and show off their aerial antics.

LEFT: A dolphin's blowhole, eyes and ears are very sensitive parts of the body. To prevent injury to JoJo, a friendly bottlenosed dolphin, Club Med erected a sign to warn guests against touching these areas.

BELOW: Human/ dolphin encounters such as this have been recorded throughout the centuries, even as far back as ancient Greece.

miles around to meet the dolphins in the knee-deep shallows of the lagoon. The dolphins allow their 'human admirers' to touch them, and as with other dolphin encounters, the dolphins prefer to interact with the children. The dolphins often take fish, offered from a friendly outstretched hand. But what really makes these encounters different from previous ones is that they are not solitary dolphins, but belong to a social group. Dolphins and people still meet at Monkey Mia, a living testimony as to how humans should live in harmony with their fellow creatures.

These are just a few examples of friendly encounters between people and dolphins. But where do they come from? And why do they behave the way they do? It has been suggested that these friendly solitary dolphins may have been banished from their own social group and are seeking company. This could be true for male solitary dolphins, but it seems unlikely that a female (and many encounters have involved females) would be banished. However, they could possibly have been separated by accident.

The Royal Navy has worked with dolphins for many years and sometimes they are let loose in open water. These animals have been trained to retrieve test equipment by homing in on a built-in acoustic signal. Some of these animals go 'absent without leave' and are never seen again. Could it be that they turn up at a later date as 'friendlies', searching out their human companions?

Many marine zoos situated on the

BELOW: Every day in a remote corner of Western Australia, humans and dolphins meet in the shallows at Monkey Mia. People travel from miles around for the opportunity to see or touch these ambassadors from the sea.

RIGHT: JoJo, a friendly dolphin, seen attacking a harmless grey nurse shark. Dolphins have been known to tackle much larger sharks, if the need arises, by ramming into the shark's gills with their hard beaks.
RIGHT: Pilot whales are one of several species of cetecean trained by the navy to retrieve test equipment from the bottom of the sea.

ABOVE: Dolphins are intensely curious and seem to enjoy a variety of new experiences. JoJo shows particular interest in a small wind-up toy, exploring it with his sonar as well as his beak.

coast use a fenced-off area of a natural lagoon or estuary as a pool. During a storm these barriers may be breached allowing a dolphin to return to the sea. Could friendly dolphins have originated from marine zoos? Some friendly dolphins in the wild will play with toys, such as balls, while others ignore them. Although solitary friendly dolphins have taken dead fish from humans, none has been observed to eat any. If they had originated from a marine zoo they would be used to balls and other such objects, and they would also be used to eating dead fish. But wherever they come from, these dolphins have provided us with a unique opportunity for humans and dolphins to meet, and with yet another mystery to unravel.

Although encounters with whales have not provided quite the same level of interaction as with dolphins, this may partly be due to the fact that most dolphin encounters involve coastal species, whereas most whales live in open waters. However, divers have swum with the larger whales. People who have encountered a whale in its own environment are immediately impressed by its sheer size and grace. On the whole, whales tend to remain at a safe distance from human divers. On those occasions when divers have entered the water in front of a group of whales, they have been observed with some interest. The whale has slowly rolled to one side so as to miss the diver and the flippers and tail flukes have been carefully lifted out of the way. These mighty creatures show no malice towards us, though we have slaughtered countless numbers of them to near extinction.

WHALE WATCHING – IN THE WILD AND IN THE ZOO

LEFT: Whale watchers delight at the sight of a humpback whale breaching. Humpback whales can be easily identified by their huge white pectoral fins.

The best way to see the larger whales is to join a whale-watching tour. There are many holiday companies that specialize in wildlife holidays and most include a whale-watching tour among them. Whale-watching tours are available in many parts ot the world, including the seas off California, Mexico, Alaska, Canada, Newfoundland, Norway and Greenland.

When most people think of whale watching, it is the grey whales (*Eschrichtius robustus*) off California which come to mind. These noble creatures migrate from their summer feeding grounds to their winter breeding grounds around California and Mexico every year.

Whale watchers in small boats are often approached by an inquisitive whale and the enthralled onlookers may even get the chance to touch a live whale. Like many of the dolphin encounters, the friendly whales are usually solitary and may be juveniles. Some of the older friendly whales may have originally approached such boats when they were younger. Often a head will pop out of the water next to a boat, showering the occupants with spray as it blows.

Grey whales are not the only species of whale that are encountered on whale-watching tours. Killer whales (*Orcinus orca*) can be seen off British Columbia and Vancouver, while minke

ABOVE: A boat full of whale watchers encounter a female grey whale in Magdalena Bay, Baja, California. As the whale watchers reach out to the whale, her calf takes in the scene with an inquisitive eye.

(*Balaenoptera acutorostrata*) and hump-back whales (*Megaptera novaeangliae*) may be seen off the coasts of New-foundland. Off the coast of Norway, it is possible to see pilot whales (*Globi-cephala*) and sperm whales (*Physeter macrocephalus*). Apart from other species of whale, dolphins and other marine life may also be observed on such tours.

Whale watching has now become big business and the whales are hunted with binoculars and cameras, instead of ex-plosive harpoons. Although not all whales are as approachable as the grey whales, whale-watching tours provide an ideal opportunity to see these mar-vellous, somewhat elusive creatures in

ABOVE: This attractively marked Pacific white-sided dolphin, seen here at San Diego Sea World California, is just one of the many species of dolphin that you may encounter on a whale watching tour.

LEFT: The narrow, high spout of the blue whale is a sight most whale watchers would love to see. These mighty leviathans may reach 33 metres (108ft) in length and weight as much as 40 adult elephants.

RIGHT: Bottlenosed dolphins, like this one seen here at Marineland San Francisco, are the dolphins usually associated with aquatic zoos and marine parks; in fact, to many people, there is only one species.

the wild. And indeed, what other animal of such size and stature could we safely approach in the wild, or even in a zoo? Yet these gentle great whales tolerate our advances and regard us with what seems to be indifference and possibly even interest. Maybe (at the risk of anthropomorphizing) they wonder just what these frail little land mammals are up to, floating in the sea with little more than a thin layer of rubber between them and the waves.

Not all of us are fortunate enough to be able to see a whale or dolphin in the wild, but there is one way that we can all see whales and dolphins closer to home, and that is at a marine zoo or ocean park. The species most frequently seen is the bottlenosed dolphin (*Tursiops truncatus*), although at some of the larger ocean parks it is also possible to see species such as the Pacific white-sided dolphin (*Lagenorhynchus obliquidas*) and killer whales, as well as seals, sealions, and other marine life.

RIGHT: At 1.3 metres (3ft 7inches), Commerson's dolphin is one of the smallest species of dolphin. Although very little is known about the biology of this animal, it is hoped that the study of these animals in marine parks will provide us with more information and a better understanding of the species.

Many marine zoos teach their animals 'trained behaviours', which are based on behaviours that the animals do naturally in the wild and provide the animals with both physical and mental exercise. Although fish forms part of the reward system, the animals also respond to petting as a reward and many marine zoos use a mixture of the two.

The basic concept of training is positive reinforcement. The animal is given a visual clue, which is usually a hand signal, and is rewarded for a correct response. If the animal does not respond correctly, no reward is given for that particular behaviour. A whistle is used to signal the end of a behaviour and acts as a bridge between behaviour and reward.

Many marine zoos provide their animals with complex interactive play sessions involving animal and trainer in random exercises which the animals seem to enjoy with no expectation of reward, other than petting and praising. Sometimes, games invented in these sessions become part of the animal demonstrations. These demonstrations are beneficial and serve as an outlet for the animal's natural playfulness. Not only do they seem to enjoy taking part in the demonstrations, but they also sem to enjoy 'pleasing' the trainer.

Although the whale's or dolphin's human keeper is called a trainer, this description is misleading, as it indicates a one-way situation where the animal is trained to learn and repeat a series of

ABOVE: Dolphin Research Centre, Grassy Key, Florida. The dolphin's natural behaviour can be modified by the trainer to produce the animal demonstrations which are seen in many aquatic zoos.

LEFT: Dolphin demonstrations play an important part in the overall educational programme of an aquatic zoo.

ABOVE: An underwater encounter between diver and cetaceans in an aquatic zoo. Many aquatic zoos have now introduced underwater interactive feeding sessons to further demonstrate the dolphins' natural abilities.

menial tricks. The relationship between animal and trainer is in fact two-way, and often the trainer learns just as much from the animal as the animal does from the trainer. The relationship is based on trust, and a new trainer must establish a strong rapport with the animals he or she works with. It is important that trainers should have a good knowledge of the animals in their charge and that they understand and record the daily natural behaviours of their animals, as these often given clues to the animals' health and condition. The behaviours that are seen in the animal demonstrations are a result of much hard work and patience on the animal's part, as well as on the part of the trainer.

Training the animals in this way is also an essential part of their general husbandry and care. For example, a whale or dolphin can be trained to present its tail so that a blood sample can be taken, which is an excellent way to monitor the animal's health. If the animals were not trained in this way, they would need to be restrained for the sample to be taken. In this situation, a sample could only be taken if there was already a problem, because this method would be stressful (and thus detrimental to the animal's well-being). By training the animal to present its tail, a blood sample is taken on a regular basis, without stress, and hopefully potential health problems can be spotted and prevented before they

RIGHT: Although dolphins possess no external ears, they do have internal ears; the earhole is visible as a small pinhole behind the eye.

BELOW: The relationships between trainer and dolphin is one based on trust. A trainer can communicate with the dolphins by teaching them simple signs and signals.

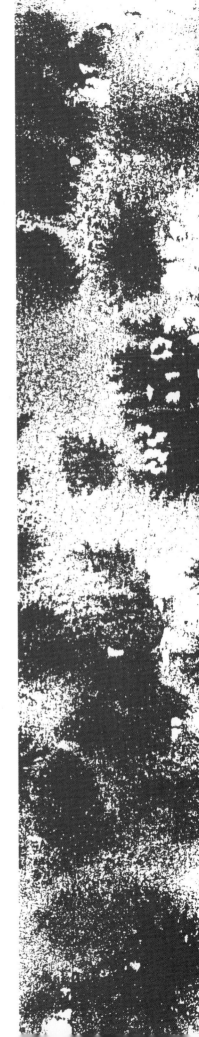

arise. Many other veterinary check-ups can be done in this way.

It is important for people to be more aware of this and other aspects of keeping and training cetaceans, as there are many misconceptions surrounding their training and general care. It is up to marine zoos to present such relevant information to their visitors, either as literature, or as part of the animal demonstrations.

Marine zoos are also becoming increasingly important as places of research, particularly for independent scientists who are able to study these animals at much closer quarters than in the wild. For example, scientists studying dolphin vocalization have been able to record their sounds using hydrophones and at the same time film their behaviours, thus enabling them to look for clues as to the meaning of their vocalizations.

Marine zoos, and in particular the animal demonstrations, have great potential for educating and informing the public. For many people, marine zoos are the only place that they will see a 'living' whale or dolphin, and nothing can replace seeing a live animal. If these animals are to survive in the wild, marine zoos and other organizations need to be able to continue to enlighten and educate people about these animals and their aquatic world, and how many of our activities are threatening their existence. However, no one animal species can be conserved if we do not protect their environment, and marine zoos are an excellent place to see and learn about a wide range of aquatic animals and how they are *all* important in the survival of our planet.

ABOVE: Occasionally, it may be necessary to move a dolphin to another pool: for instance, for a veterinary check-up. This is done by using a specifically constructed stretcher, as seen here.

RIGHT: A dolphin petting pool gives visitors a unique opportunity, not only to touch a dolphin, but also to learn about them first hand from an experienced staff member, who is always nearby.

EIGHT

THE KILLING
OF WHALES

LEFT: Hvalf
Jordur, Iceland.
Advances in man's
technology
transformed the
hunting of whales
from a heroic deed
to one of mass
slaughter.

BELOW, LEFT AND OPPOSITE: Depictions of whaling in *The Fisheries of the World* by F. Whymper, published in London by Cassell & Co. Ltd in 1883.

The history of whaling is a long and bloody one and has its origins deeply rooted in our past. Coastal communities possibly utilized the carcasses of dead whales long before commercial whaling began, and having discovered uses for dead whales, it seems a likely progression for humans to hunt actively live whales. At this time, the most important products from whaling were oil made from their blubber, and stiffening for garments and umbrellas made from whalebone. The whale meat may have been eaten if the whale had not been long dead. Whales may have been beached alive, but were not approached until it was certain that they were no longer living.

The first whale killed by humans could well have been such an animal, stranded in shallow water. In these early times, whales were thought of as

fearsome sea monsters, and so to kill such an animal would have been considered a very heroic deed.

Early whaling originated only to support the needs of the local community. Bowhead (*Balaena mysticetus*) and right whales (*Eubalaena glacialis*) were the first species to be hunted, the right whale receiving its name because it was a slow swimmer and floated when dead, making it the 'right' whale to hunt. Whaling slowly spread through Europe and Asia and became more and more a large commercial industry, rather than a subsistence hunting exercise.

By the sixteenth century, Holland and the UK started whaling in arctic waters. By the seventeenth century, North American whalers had started to hunt the right and humpback whales as they followed their migrations.

But whaling was still limited by technology. Whaling operations were land-based and slaughtered whales had to be towed ashore or cut up next to the ship. Whales were killed with hand-held harpoons fired from small rowing boats launched from the sailing ships. The Japanese also started whaling in the seventeenth century, although their method involved using small boats and nets.

As technology and ship design improved, whalers were able to pursue other species, particularly the sperm whale (*Physeter macrocephalus*). During the eighteenth century and the early part of the nineteenth century, whalers penetrated deeper into arctic waters and soon overfishing caused the total collapse of the arctic whaling industry around the beginning of the nineteenth century.

In the middle of the nineteenth century, two new inventions were destined to increase greatly the efficiency of the whaling industry. The first of these inventions was the steam-driven ship. Whalers soon became equipped with a fleet of steam-driven vessels, allowing them to reach new whaling grounds and pursue faster species such as the rorquals – the blue *(Balaenoptera musculus)*, fin *(B. physalus)* and sei *(B. borealis)* whales in particular.

The second invention was to bring about even-greater change. The explosive harpoon gun, which was mounted on the bow of the new whaling ships, fired a harpoon which trailed a powerful line behind it. The harpoon hit the whale with such force that the tip was driven deep into the body, and four barbs prevented it from being pulled free. The harpoon was also equipped with explosives which detonated inside the whale. Often the harpoon hit a fleshy part of the body and caused a slow, painful death, sometimes lasting two hours.

The year 1924 saw the first factory ship in operation. They were first introduced by the Norwegians, the factory ship being served by a fleet of smaller catcher boats. Whalers were no longer tied to a land base, and harpooned whales could be hauled on to the decks and processed. All parts of the whale were now saved for use: the oil from blubber, the tongue and meat for human consumption or animal feed; and anything that was left over was ground down to make fertilizer. Nothing was wasted – except the whale itself.

Whaling was no longer a heroic adventure, as the excitement and danger had been totally removed by the

BELOW: Following the invention of the steam driven ship, whalers were able to hunt the faster swimming rorquals and the blue, fin and sei whales. The sei whale, pictured below, is much smaller than the blue and fin whales and so was not hunted in lage numbers until stocks of the two larger species had been greatly reduced.

LEFT: As the explosive harpoon hits the whale, it is driven deep into its body by the impact. The sea condition often does not allow an accurate enough shot to ensure the harpoon hits a vulnerable area. In these cases, the whale takes much longer to die.

use of explosive harpoons and floating processing plants. In short, whaling had become mass slaughter. It was stepped up with no real thought or regard for future stocks, the general assumption being that the sea would always be full of whales.

The blue whale was a prime target for whalers, as it was the largest of all the species. As the larger blues disappeared, smaller and younger whales were taken, reducing the possibility that the whales could continue to replace their diminishing numbers. As the blues became scarce, whalers turned their attention to the smaller rorquals, namely the fin whale and the sei whale.

It was finally recognized that whaling could not continue in its present state without eventually causing its own self-destruction. In 1964 the International Whaling Commission (IWC) was

RIGHT: A sad end to a mighty leviathan – another victim of mankind's greed and ignorance.

LEFT: At around 24 metres (78.8 feet), the fin whale is the second largest species of whale. Their numbers have been greatly reduced by commercial whaling and they are classified as being vulnerable to extinction. Even so, small numbers are still taken every year.

BELOW: Whalers wre able to locate whales by watching for their spout, and their appearance was heralded by a shout from the lookout. The spout from the whale pictured below identifies it as a fin whale.

formed to help preserve whales as a natural resource by protecting them from overfishing. Originally represented by 16 whaling nations, its aim was to regulate whaling activities and agree quotas for whale catches. By managing this natural resource carefully, depleted stocks would be able to recover by only taking from species that could naturally sustain themselves. Calves and females with calves were to be protected and the right whale was to receive worldwide protection.

The quota for rorquals was based on what was known as the blue whale unit, with one blue whale unit equalling either one blue whale, two fin whales, two-and-a-half humpback whales, or six sei whales. This unit reflected the

expected oil yield of each whale species, and had little regard for whether a species was endangered or not.

Many cultures, including Eskimos and Inuits, have always owed their survival to hunting marine mammals. These people were allowed to continue to take whales, even an agreed number of protected species, such as the bowhead and right whales.

In theory, by regulating the whaling industry, there should always be enough whales to replace depleted stocks. But although the International Whaling Commission was empowered to make recommendations, it did not have the power to enforce them – this decision was made by the individual member's government. There was no law to say that all whaling nations had to belong to the International Whaling Commission, and many of those that did, had the power to veto suggestions on quotas and protected species made by other countries.

Because of this, most of the rules were a compromise, and many were worse than useless. Sanctuaries for whales were created in areas where it was not viable to whale anyway, and minimum-size limits did not allow for individual whales to reproduce and rear their young before becoming a target for whaling, thus greatly reducing the likelihood of a whale species holding its own (in terms of numbers) against the slaughter.

Until the late 1960s, it was only large species of cetacean that were slaughtered. But it was around this time that the tuna fisheries changed from rod and line fishing to using purse seine nets. Tuna fishermen have always known that dolphins and tuna fish swim together. Both tuna fish and dolphins feed on small fish, and as the tuna fish feed, some of the small fish are driven up to the waiting dolphins and vice versa. As it is easier to spot the dolphins than it is the tuna, the fishermen started to set their nets around the schools of dolphins. As well as trapping the fish, the nets also trapped the dolphins, most of which drowned. The dead dolphins were dumped back in the sea while the nets were hauled aboard.

It wasn't until the end of the 1960s that the public became aware of the dolphins' plight. Also at this time, there came about a change in the public's attitude towards cetaceans. Concern from conservationists and the public led to the forming of the US Marine Mammal Protection Act in 1972, which forbade the killing or taking of marine mammals in US waters without a special

BELOW: Early whalers often engraved whaling scenes on the teeth of harpooned sperm whales; this is known as scrimshaw. The whalers probably sold their scrimshaw when they returned to port. This is a piece of local scrimshaw from the Azores.

LEFT: A tiger shark in Hawaiian waters, feeding on the carcass of a harpooned whale. If a great deal of blood is present in the water, it may trigger a feeding frenzy amongst the sharks.

RIGHT: Whale meat is still eaten in some countries, particularly Japan and Iceland. Whale meat that is not fit for human consumption goes to make animal feed.

permit, and which also covered products made from marine mammals. However, the Fisheries Department did not recognize this legislation and allowed the tuna fisheries to continue killing dolphins in their fishing nets.

The National Marine Fisheries Service was eventually forced to act on this situation. A new design for tuna fish nets was introduced which allowed dolphins to be freed from the nets, but this could not be effectively enforced and it was left up to individual fishermen whether dolphins were freed or not. The US Protection Act also brought into force what was considered to be an 'acceptable' level of dolphin deaths caused by tuna fishing.

Also in the late 1970s, the United Nations Conference for the Human Environment called for a 10-year moratorium on whaling, but this was not accepted by the International Whaling Commission. Environmental groups such as Greenpeace and the World Wide Fund for Nature campaigned for a total ban on whaling. Greenpeace members put themselves in the thick of the action by using small inflatable boats to position themselves between the whaling ships and their quarry, only this time heroism was on the side of the whale. Other pressure groups also whipped up public support and sympathy for the whales.

Many scientists expressed their concern over the problem of assessing the size of whale populations and how much exploitation they could withstand. By now, the public had had the chance to meet dolphins and whales in marine zoos and found them to be clever, in-telligent mammals. So possibly their larger cousins, the great whales, deserved a better fate than the whaler's harpoon and the large flensing knives.

Eventually the hard work of campaigners and other concerned people paid off. In 1982, a ban on commercial whaling was agreed and was to take effect from 1986. At last it appeared that a victory had been achieved and that the whales had been saved from the jaws of extinction at the final hour. But was it a victory or a postponement?

The 10-year ban on whaling was to scientists a chance to study whale populations and assess the possibilities for the future of whaling. However, a provision in the moratorium allowed the catching of whales for scientific purposes by special permit – even protected species. Iceland and South Korea stopped commercial whaling and started scientific whaling. The whalers expressed their reasons as being necessary

BELOW: A rorqual being processed by whalers on an Icelandic factory ship. With the advent of the factory ship in 1924, whales could be processed at sea, enabling whalers to kill more whales.

to provide data on whale stocks, but was it just a coincidence that the whale meat was sold to Japan? Japan and Norway also expressed their intentions of starting scientific whaling.

Although commercial whaling has ceased, non-commercial whaling or aboriginal whaling for subsistence is legal. Some of this whaling is still done in the traditional way, using a hand-held harpoon, although many have now introduced the use of guns and outboard motors.

Pilot whales have been hunted by the people of the Faeroe Islands for over 500 years. The whales are herded into traditional shallow bays by a method known as drive fishing, where they are killed by gaffing or stabbing, usually from small boats. Pilot whales are an ideal quarry for drive fisheries as they live in close social units. Drive-

whale fisheries also occur off the Hebrides and off the Orkney and Shetland Islands, where the whale oil is important for lighting.

Studies on drive fisheries have shown that the many whales that approach these traditional bays may be using geomagnetic contours to help them navigate. As they come within range of the bay, the islanders chase the whales towards shore where they are killed. It has been shown that a frightened whale will flee in any direction which has no relation to the geomagnetic contours.

So far, it is thought that these fisheries pose no real threat to whales on the worldwide scale that commercial whaling has. However, the question to address is, can we really justify even a traditional hunt with no other reason than that it's been happening for hundreds of years?

THE
CONTINUING
IMPACT OF
HUMANS

LEFT: A friendly
encounter with a
grey whale
*(Eschrichtius
robustus).*

Until recently, commercial whaling was by far the greatest threat to cetaceans. Now that it has ceased, one could easily be forgiven for thinking that their future was secure. But whales and dolphins are now threatened by many of our other activities, including fishing and pollution from industry and agriculture.

By far the most immediate threat is the fishing method known as gill net fishing. Gill netting is a very efficient way of catching fish, but unfortunately, it also kills large numbers of turtles, seabirds, non-commercial fish, dolphins, whales and many other marine mammals. There are two types of gill netting activity: the pelagic drift net fishing (it has been estimated that thousands of miles of nets are used worldwide); and coastal fixed gill nets.

What impact this has on world populations of cetaceans is unknown, but clearly more research into incidental deaths in gill nets is needed before recommendations can be made. Recent research has been done to find out why cetaceans, many of which have superb echolocation ability, become entangled in gill nets in the first place. Studies on the sound production and reception of the bottlenosed dolphin (*Tursiops truncatus*) has revealed that when they use their echolocation ability for hunt-

ABOVE: Many dolphins drown when they become entangled in fishing nets, which are by far the most immediate threat to both dolphins and whales today.

ing prey, they concentrate on one fish which they pursue, disregarding the other fish in the shoal. The returning echo from the fish is strong, and echoes from the other fish are ignored. Weaker echoes from their surroundings are also ignored, including the weak echo that would return from fishing nets, so the dolphin may not be aware of the net until it is too late.

Baleen whales – mainly minke whales (*Balaenoptera acutorostrata*), humpack whales (*Megaptera novaeangliae*) and fin whales (*B. physalus*) – may blunder into nets by mistake. This may also be a problem with whales that navigate by following geomagnetic contours, as these routes have to be learnt, and the whale may come up against netting that was not there on a previous excursion.

The Japanese North Pacific salmon fishery consists of two fishing fleets which between them let out 20,000 m (66,000 ft) of drift gill netting each night. As well as catching salmon, about 2,300 Dall's porpoise (*Phocoenoides dalli*) are entangled each year. Inshore netting also results in the entanglement of 25,000 small cetaceans each year, mainly Pacific white-sided dolphins (*Lagenorhynchus obliquidens*) and harbour porpoise (*Phocoena phocoena*). The Vaquita, or Gulf of California harbour porpoise (*Phocoena sinus*) is extremely vulnerable to entanglement in fishing nets because of its small and localized population.

Research is being undertaken to assess the possibility of using some form of acoustic device attached to the nets

BELOW: The Pacific white-sided dolphin, found in the Pacific Ocean, is but one of many species of dolphin that is incidentally killed in fishing nets each year.

to warn whales and dolphins of their presence. This may reduce some entanglements, but it is thought that some species of small cetacean, particularly porpoises, may be attracted to the nets by the abundance of trapped fish and become entangled themselves.

Although the number of small cetaceans killed in nets may not seem very high, the victims are often from small localized populations which may be easily decimated. While it is difficult to assess the effects on worldwide populations, what is certain is that ways must be found to reduce incidental killing of marine mammals.

River dolphins are also victims of gill netting. The La Plata River dolphin (*Pontoporia blainvillei*) is taken incidentally by gill net fisheries in Brazil, Uruguay and Argentina; a similar fate is met by the Amazon River dolphin (*Inia geoffrensis*) and tucuxi (*Sotalia fluviatilis*) in fisheries on the Amazon

ABOVE: There are five species of river dolphin; all are threatened by nets, boat traffic and river development. The most endangered species of dolphin is the Yangtse River dolphin, which may number only a few hundred.

and its tributaries. The Amazon River dolphin is also killed for its oil and its eyes, which are sold in the local market and tourist shops as good luck charms.

Although a moratorium exists for commercial whaling, this only covers the great whales. Many of the smaller cetacean species are also exploited, and even though most are taken for subsistence, populations of these cetaceans can just as easily be overfished. Not only are pilot whales taken in drive fisheries, but the narwal (*Monodon monoceros*) and the beluga (*Delphinapterus leucas*) are also hunted in some parts of their range, often using modern technology.

There is a very real fear that incidental catches of small cetaceans may develop into an established major

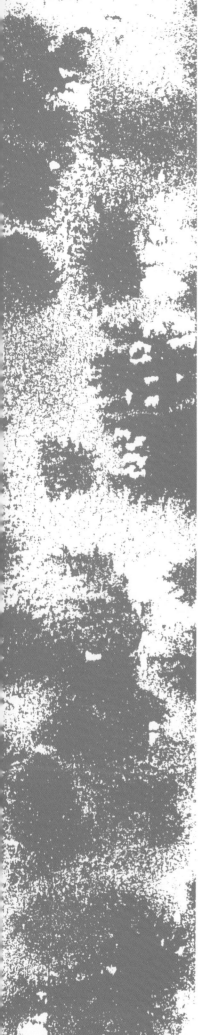

fishery. As the supplies of whale meat to Japan run out, will they be replaced with meat from small cetaceans? Japan is already responsible for a large proportion of existing fisheries of small cetaceans. These animals are harpooned from small boats, and many species are involved, including Baird's Beaked whale (*Berardius bairdi*), the pilot whale and Dall's porpoise. Some 33,000 of the latter were taken in 1988.

Where people and cetaceans compete for the same food, problems will always occur. Whales and dolphins are often blamed for damaging nets, scaring fish or eating them, which on occasions have led to the animals being culled. The dolphin culls at Iki Island have received much publicity in the past. The dolphins, which included bottlenosed dolphins and Pacific white-sided dolphins, were blamed for a decline in fish catches. The culled dolphins were ground up and processed for animal feed.

Experiments have been undertaken into the use of an acoustic 'scarecrow'. Scientists played killer whale sounds through underwater microphones in an area where dolphins conflicted with fishing operations. As killer whales sometimes feed on smaller cetaceans, it was thought that the recordings would scare off the dolphins from around the fisheries, thus protecting the nets, the fishermen's livelihood and the dolphins from becoming the victims of a legal (or illegal) cull. At this stage the success and practicability of these experiments has yet to be determined.

Krill, a swarming shrimp-like crustacean, forms an important part of the staple diet of many baleen whale species.

Krill is found mainly in cold waters where there is a good food supply, and it is not at all surprising that many baleen whale species spend their summer feeding in polar waters. However, several nations are considering fishing for krill; indeed, the USSR and Japan already have krill fishing fleets. The real question is, can krill support the whales, seals, penguins and seabirds that rely on it for food and provide humans with a sustainable catch? Could we now be in danger of starving the whales that we have struggled to protect from the whalers?

Small cetaceans face so many threats that it is impossible to name them all. Small cetaceans, namely dolphins and porpoises, are illegally killed by harpoon to provide crab bait for the Chilean crab fishery. The Ganges River dolphin (*Platanista gangetica*) suffers a similar fate to the La Plata River dolphin, as it is hunted for its oil which is then used by fishermen to lure catfish into their nets. An Action Plan for the conservation of whales, dolphins and porpoises for 1988–1992 has been drawn up for the International Union for Conservation of Nature and National Resources (IUCN) by its cetacean specialist group which deals with these and many other issues affecting cetaceans – including possible solutions (see reference list).

Whales and dolphins are also affected indirectly by many of our activities. Raw, untreated sewage is still dumped into our seas, which can cause great harm to the environment. It has been estimated that 1,400 million litres (300 million gallons) of sewage is dumped into UK waters almost every day. Sew-

LEFT: Toxic chemicals such as PCBs (polychlorinated biphenyls) are absorbed by the blubber of whales, dolphins and other marine mammals. Although we do not yet know what effect this may have on cetaceans, research on seals has shown it to cause reproductive failure.

age provides food for the many bacteria that live in the sea, which multiply in their thousands to exploit this new food source. Unfortunately, however, these masses of bacteria greatly deplete the oxygen level in the water, thus depriving many benthic (bottom-living) animals of oxygen and disrupting the food chain. Coastal waters may become lifeless, which could also affect coastal species of whales and dolphins. There is also an obvious health risk to humans. The main problem with sewage disposal in the UK is that most of the system is Victorian and not designed to cope with the large quantities disposed of today. If the sewage could be treated before being disposed of through longer outfalls, it would be far less harmful.

ABOVE: Many thousand Dall's porpoises are killed each year in fishing nets, whilst many others are harpooned from small boats. Although they are not yet considered to be threatened, they may well be in the future if they are not protected.

ABOVE: At 11 metres (36.1 feet), the minke whale is the smallest of the rorquals. Large numbers of minke whales are still killed each year under the guise of scientific whaling.

However, sewage treatment plants are expensive to build, and one would be needed by almost every major seaside town. What price are we prepared to pay for cleaner seas?

The coastal habitat is also being destroyed in other ways. Much of our natural coastland is being replaced by marinas, harbours and other new development. Again, its effects on the local habitat may also affect the higher members of the food chain, including whales and dolphins. The river dolphins are probably the most vulnerable to development. Many species are threatened by the erection of dams and tidal

RIGHT: The right whale is thought to be the most endangered species of great whale. It is feared that pollution of the seas may be the final nail in their coffin.

barrages, which often separate populations of river dolphins or affect their food.

Our contamination of the seas with chemicals may be a threat to all marine life. Most of this contamination comes from farming (chemicals which are washed or blown into the sea) and from industry, although some also come from coastal communities. By far the most dangerous chemicals which have found their way into the marine food chain are the polychlorinated biphenyls, or PCBs as they are generally known.

PCBs are fat-soluble and do not dissolve in water; therefore they accumulate in the fatty tissues of marine animals. Small quantities of PCBs present in the lower animals are greatly increased in the higher animals that feed on them; therefore the higher up the food chain, the higher the quantities of PCBs present. For this reason, toothed whales and dolphins are at a greater risk than the baleen whales that are lower down in the food chain. Even a lactating female whale or dolphin can pass the chemicals on to her calf as her fat reserves are turned into milk.

So far we do not know what damage, if any, these chemicals may cause to whales and dolphins, but research on seals has shown that PCBs cause reproductive failure. Although PCB production has been phased out, two-thirds of the PCBs that have been manufactured have yet to be disposed of. So far, the only method found for destroying PCBs is in the intense heat of specially constructed incinerators, of which there are only a few in existence. It has been suggested that if we continue to dump pollutants into the sea, by 1999, fish

and shellfish may be so polluted as to make them unfit for human consumption. We can change our diet, but what choice do the whales, dolphins and other marine mammals have? Countries whose people have high quantities of fish in their diets may be affected first.

Whales and dolphins that have survived the long and bloodied slaughters by the whalers may now be threatened by these invisible killers. Like many other events in the past, it is not until the situation has become almost irreversible that we acknowledge that a problem exists. Many of these toxins are so well established in the food chain that even if we were to ban all these chemicals today, they would still remain in the environment for many years, and it will be even longer before the damage they have done can be repaired.

Noise pollution, such as that produced by shipping and underwater seismic testing for oil and other minerals, may also affect whales and dolphins. Although there is no evidence to show that it disturbs cetaceans, it may at the very least deter friendly dolphins. It is believed that the larger great whales could at one time communicate to each other over vast distances, possibly across a whole ocean or more. Sound pollution is thought to mask these sound signals and reduce the distance that these sounds can be heard today.

With the increase in boat traffic, there is also a greater chance of collisions occurring between boats and cetaceans. Again, it is the rare freshwater river dolphins that are at most risk as their river habitats become further developed by humans.

WHAT THE
FUTURE
HOLDS

LEFT: Pacific
spotted dolphins in
Hawaiian waters.
Pacific spotted
dolphins are one of
several species of
dolphin that often
associate with tuna
fish, which results in
the accidental death
of thousands of
these dolphins each
year in tuna fishing
nets.

LEFT: An engraving
from *Giant Fishes,
Whales and Dolphins*
by J. R. Norman and
F. C. Fraser,
published in London
in 1937.

FIG. 60.—Greenland Right Whale (*Balæna mysticetus*). To 60 feet.

FIG. 61.—Black Right Whale (*Balæna glacialis*). To 60 feet.

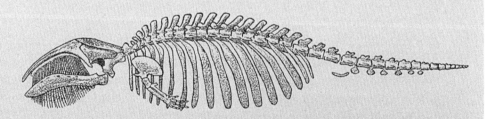

FIG. 62.—Skeleton of Pigmy Right Whale (*Neobalæna marginata*). To 20 feet.

ABOVE: Scientists are able to learn a great deal about whales by using benign methods of research. Here a scientist is using a biopsy dart to take a skin sample from a humpback whale.

Many species of whale and dolphin are already known to be endangered or vulnerable, and many others may soon be added to the list. The Yangtse River dolphin (*Lipotes vexillifer*) is considered to be the most endangered of all the cetaceans as only a few hundred are thought to remain. Only a few are killed each year, usually incidentally in nets and by boat traffic, but even this may have a great impact on such a small population.

The northern right whale (*Eubalaena glacialis*) is thought to be the most endangered species of baleen whale. The right whale and the bowhead whale

(*Balaena mysticetus*) were the first species to be targeted by commercial whaling, and they too are both rare. The great whales' recovery has been greatly hindered by their slow reproductive rate. Many species congregate during the breeding season, but for the rest of the year they are widely spread and some individuals may find it increasingly hard to find a mate. Some species, such as the humpack whale (*Megaptera novaeangliae*) and the blue whale (*Balaenoptera musculus*), are divided into separate geographical populations which rarely, if ever, meet. An added problem facing these species

ABOVE: Scientists have learned much about the private lives of whales and dolphins by studying the sounds that they make in relation to the behaviours recorded. The scientist seen here is recording the sounds of humpback whales.

saur, whose massive tongue alone weighs as much as a bull elephant, may soon disappear forever.

Many centuries ago, when sailors believed the sea to be inhabited by sea monsters, whales were killed in acts of valour. Oil was extracted from their blubber and used for lighting and the manufacture of soaps, margarines and other food stuffs. Their meat was eaten in a few countries; in others it was processed into animal feed or fertilizer. Their bones were even used to make corsets and later to make glue. At least we can understand why the whales were killed. But today, knowing that all their products can be made artificially or found elsewhere, and knowing them to be gentle, intelligent creatures, what right have we to continue to shed their blood? Even the spermaceti oil from the great sperm whale (*Physeter macrocephalus*), that is used as a high-quality lubricant and wax, can be replaced with oil from jojoba, a shrub found in the deserts of central America. Jojoba can also be used in the manufacture of many products, including glues, plastics and soaps.

Some countries have continued whaling, in the guise of 'scientific whaling', but the whale meat is still sold commercially. Very little, if any, benefit can be obtained from a butchered whale. But valuable research is being carried out on whales and dolphins in the field by dedicated scientists and researchers using benign methods of investigation. These researchers have gathered a wide range of data, without harming a single whale.

Scientists are able to identify individual whales by their unique natural

is inbreeding which could eventually weaken breeding stocks, causing them to die out.

Although the blue whale (*Balaenoptera musculus*) has been snatched from the edge of extinction, it has little chance of recovering its original numbers of 150,000 or more. At present, the blue whale population is thought to be between 10,000 and 15,000. These mighty leviathans, whose immense size exceeds that of the largest known dino-

RIGHT: The future of this juvenile humpback whale does not look too bright. Although humpbacks are protected from commercial whaling, mankind continues to treat the seas as his own private dumping grounds with little concern or regard for their inhabitants.

markings. By recording these markings, researchers have been able to study the social interaction between members of a pod of whales. The natural markings can also be used to study the movements of different pods, as again, they can be recognized by identifying one or more individuals in the group. Scientists have even been able to determine what some species of whale feed on, without having to kill the subject. The sperm whale often defecates before a deep dive. By netting samples of faeces from the water, and by studying partially digested squid and squid beaks, it has been possible to identify several species of squid prey.

Cetacean vocalization can now be studied using modern technology, and perhaps one day we shall unravel the meaning of their strange sounds. Roger Payne has already made many recordings of humpback whale vocalizations, and with the aid of field observations, is working towards an understanding of the humpback's eerie, haunting song.

Whale observation posts have been set up, many in remote areas, to identify and record the movements of whales and dolphins. Some organizations encourge the public to participate in whale- and dolphin-watch schemes, and often involve fishermen, divers and people who live near the coast.

ABOVE: The common dolphin is the species most frequently seen riding the bow wave of ships. The sea would surely be a desolate place without these fun-loving creatures.

RIGHT: Being a coastal species, the bottlenosed dolphin is thought to be a victim of coastal pollution as well as falling foul of fishing nets. If we do not change our attitudes towards the oceans, the only cetaceans left in the world will be those in aquatic zoos.

One small glimmer of hope that countries may learn to work together to protect the environment came in the guise of three grey whales (*Eschrichtius robustus*): Crossbeak, Bonnet and Bone. In October 1988, these three whales became trapped in the ice, off the coast of north Alaska near the town of Barrow. After more than two weeks of combined effort between Americans, Russians and local Eskimos, two of the three whales escaped to freedom. Sadly, Bone, the smallest of the whales, never made it. The story was followed by concerned well-wishers all over the world and the plight of these three whales touched the hearts of millions. The whales had become trapped due to an early freeze, a few miles from the open water. If such cooperation could be mobilized to save three whales, think what could be achieved if all countries cooperated to conserve wildlife.

Although the great whales received protection through the 10-year moratorium, many of the smaller species of cetacean were overlooked. The Action Plan for the IUCN was drawn up to assess the threats, particularly to those smaller species, and recommend a plan of action. Many priority schemes have been outlined, but funding will be needed to carry them out.

Many of the problems that whales and dolphins face are widespread, and many go on almost unnoticed in the poorer developing countries. For the same reason, it is hard to assess accurately the level of the problem, and therefore even harder to regulate. The destruction of the environment is often subtle and goes along unnoticed for many years.

Large amounts of pollutants and toxic chemicals, some of which have been dumped illegally, are present in the sea and in the bodies of many marine organisms. Only international cooperation regarding these issues can provide any hope of improvement. Many of these chemicals affect all levels of the food chain, including cetaceans and the animals they eat. No one animal can be conserved if we do not protect the environment it lives in. Only now are we beginning to realize that we cannot continue to dispose of unwanted chemicals in this way without paying for the consequences.

As pollution of the oceans tends to be a less emotive subject than whaling, it is proving to be much harder to generate the same concern and public support for its control. However, marine pollution was brought to the public's attention in 1989 when it was blamed for the cause of a mysterious virus which killed over 17,000 seals off the coasts of Europe. We do not know what long-term effects such pollution may have on whales and dolphins, but it is thought that it reduces the animals' natural immunities.

Until a recent law was introduced prohibiting the disposal of waste material at sea by shipping, approximately 100,000 marine mammals and two million seabirds were thought to be killed each year by marine refuse. Hopefully this new law will at least reduce the problem. But clearly what is needed is an international law of the seas, which must be observed by all countries, regarding the control of sewage pollution, toxic waste, refuse, fishing operations and all other exploitations of the marine

environment. Many countries, including the UK, are taking positive steps forward by setting up voluntary marine reserves, which are managed by the local council and other users of the area, such as fishermen, yachting and diving clubs. Although they have no official power, it does mean that the areas are preserved for wildlife and human activities.

Fisheries will always exist as long as there are fish in the sea to be caught. However, much more can and should be done to reduce the incidental catches of cetaceans, whether by sonic devices, stricter controls where endangered species are caught, or by restricting certain fishing methods or practices. We cannot continue to put profit before the welfare of whales and dolphins.

Estuaries in the UK support 1.5 million wading birds who spend their winters on the biologically rich mudflats. This figure represents 40% of all the wading birds that overwinter in the whole of Europe, but almost all of the UK estuaries are threatened, either by pollution or development. About half of all the wetlands in the UK have disappeared because of pollution, drainage schemes and land development in the last 40 years, threatening the existence of many rare animal and plant species.

LEFT: Pilot whales are a very social species and often form quite large herds. These whales are still hunted by drive fisheries in the Faroe Islands and are most frequently involved in mass strandings.

LEFT: The great white shark is another creature threatened by over-fishing. Many large specimens are taken by trophy hunters and sports fishermen, causing the large breeding females to become very scarce.

On a worldwide scale, 40 hectares (100 acres) of tropical rain forest are cut down every 60 seconds. The destruction of the last ancient forests also threatens many animal and plant species, many of which have not yet been discovered. We risk losing the opportunity to discover natural cures for many of our untreatable diseases. More importantly, the forests are nature's way of removing the large quantities of carbon dioxide in the air, caused by the burning of fossil fuels. The destruction of the forests will also cause drastic changes in the world's climate.

Many of our beautiful coral reefs are threatened, not just by souvenir trade, but also by pollution and industrial development. The seven species of marine turtle have become very rare, largely due to animal trade, which still persists today. Breeding beaches are disturbed by tourism, and turtles choke on polythene bags, mistaken for jelly fish, their natural prey. And as if this wasn't enough, scientists are now finding increasing signs of human pollution in the last wilderness, Antarctica. Even the great white shark, the so-called terror of the sea, is thought to be declining due to sports fishing and trophy hunters.

These are just a few of the problems facing the natural world. Many of the problems are so vast and concern so many different countries, that only international government action can change the course of destruction. It is up to us all to make our feelings known to those we elect to power.

The damage that we do to the environment will eventually affect us all. This is why it is important for us to learn and understand more about the natural world. If we cannot live in harmony with nature, what chance do we, or any other species, have for the future? The choice is ours.

RIGHT: Dolphins and humans together point the way to a better future, to a time when we will leave behind our blooded past.

GLOSSARY

BALEEN Bristly plate of whalebone with which some varieties of whale filter krill while feeding.

BREACHING Behaviour in which whales leap partly or entirely from the water.

BUBBLE NETTING Feeding technique in which whales circle below food organisms while rising to the surface, expelling air all the while to create a chain of bubble that trap the prey, thus enabling them to be easily swallowed.

ECHOLOCATION A process of emitting souds and analysing the returning echoes, used to gain information about the surrounding environment.

FLUKE One of the lobes of a whale's tail.

KRILL The mass of tiny crustaceans that provide the principle food for some whale species.

LOBTAILING Behaviour pattern found amongst whales. The whale hangs head down in the water with its flukes in the air. The whale swings its tail to and fro before slapping it down on the water.

MELON A bulbous form on the head containing fat, muscles and nasal passage and sacs.

POD Relatively stable groupings of whales, which appear to be made up of animals related to each other.

SPERMACETI OIL A wax-like substance thought to help in adjusting buoyancy during deep dives.

SPY HOPPING Behaviour (possibly a hunting technique) in which whales thrust their heads and upper bodies above the surface to inspect their surroundings.

THROAT PLEATS Grooves in the throat region of some whale species that permit expansion of the throat while feeding.

PICTURE CREDITS AND ACKNOWLEDGEMENTS

l = left; r = right; t = top; b = bottom

AGE FOTOSTOCK: front cover inset; pages 6, 11, 14 t, 16, 17 b, 23, 24, 25 t, 30, 34, 35, 44, 56 t, 65, 71, 79 b, 84 t, 79 l, 88 t, 89, 94, 95 t, 96, 98 b, 99, 105, 108, 113, 118, 121.

HEATHER ANGEL: pages 7, 17 t, 20, 39, 52 b, 82, 83 b.

KEITH BANISTER: pages 8, 10, 11, 18 b, 25 b, 28, 52 t, 68, 90 t, 90 b, 91, 114.

NELIO BARROS: page 69.

BRUCE COLEMAN LIMITED: main front cover picture.

GREENPEACE: pages 40, 48, 49, 81, 100, 102, 109.

FRANK LANE PICTURE AGENCY: pages 19, 46, 54 b, 58, 66–67, 83 t, 84 b, 95 b, 101, 110, 111.

NED MIDDLETON: page 86.

NHPA: page 3.

DOUG PERRINE: pages 1, 9, 12, 15 t, 15 b, 22, 27, 36, 38, 41, 45, 50, 55 t, 71, 73, 74, 75 t, 75 b, 76, 77 t, 77 b, 79 t, 80, 85 r, 87 b, 88 b, 115, 116, 119, 124.

PLANET EARTH PICTURES: back cover; pages 37, 47, 51, 54 t, 55 b, 70, 78, 87 t, 92, 93 t, 93 b, 97, 98 t, 104, 117, 122, 123.

STEPHEN SAVAGE: pages 14 b, 18 t, 21, 29, 31, 32, 103, 107.

OSWALDO VASQUEZ/CIBIMA: page 26.

The author gratefully acknowledges the assistance of Dr Margaret Klinowska, particularly for her contribution to the species list.

INDEX

Note: page numbers in *italics*
refer to illustrations